Cambridge Elements

Elements in Quantitative and Computational Methods for the Social Sciences
edited by
R. Michael Alvarez
*California Institute of Technology*
Nathaniel Beck
*New York University*

# TARGET ESTIMATION AND ADJUSTMENT WEIGHTING FOR SURVEY NONRESPONSE AND SAMPLING BIAS

Devin Caughey
*Massachusetts Institute of Technology*
Adam J. Berinsky
*Massachusetts Institute of Technology*
Sara Chatfield
*University of Denver*
Erin Hartman
*University of California, Los Angeles*
Eric Schickler
*University of California, Berkeley*
Jasjeet S. Sekhon
*University of California, Berkeley*

CAMBRIDGE UNIVERSITY PRESS

CAMBRIDGE
UNIVERSITY PRESS

University Printing House, Cambridge CB2 8BS, United Kingdom

One Liberty Plaza, 20th Floor, New York, NY 10006, USA

477 Williamstown Road, Port Melbourne, VIC 3207, Australia

314–321, 3rd Floor, Plot 3, Splendor Forum, Jasola District Centre,
New Delhi – 110025, India

79 Anson Road, #06–04/06, Singapore 079906

Cambridge University Press is part of the University of Cambridge.

It furthers the University's mission by disseminating knowledge in the pursuit of education, learning, and research at the highest international levels of excellence.

www.cambridge.org
Information on this title: www.cambridge.org/9781108794152
DOI: 10.1017/9781108879217



First published 2020

*A catalogue record for this publication is available from the British Library.*

ISBN 978-1-108-79415-2 Paperback
ISSN 2398-4023 (online)
ISSN 2514-3794 (print)

Additional resources for this publication at www.cambridge.org/Caughey.

# Target Estimation and Adjustment Weighting for Survey Nonresponse and Sampling Bias

Elements in Quantitative and Computational Methods for the Social Sciences

DOI: 10.1017/9781108879217
First published online: September 2020

---

Devin Caughey
*Massachusetts Institute of Technology*
Adam J. Berinsky
*Massachusetts Institute of Technology*
Sara Chatfield
*University of Denver*
Erin Hartman
*University of California, Los Angeles*
Eric Schickler
*University of California, Berkeley*
Jasjeet S. Sekhon
*University of California, Berkeley*

**Author for correspondence:** Devin Caughey, caughey@mit.edu

**Abstract:** Nonresponse and other sources of bias are endemic features of public opinion surveys. Consequently, even for probability samples, basing inferences on the sampling design alone is rarely the best option. Both the bias and the variance of design-based estimators can be reduced through the use of adjustment weights, which incorporate auxiliary information on the composition of the target population. We elaborate a general workflow of weighting-based inference, decomposing it into two main tasks. The first is the estimation of population targets from one or more sources of auxiliary information. The second is the construction of weights that calibrate the survey sample to the population targets. We emphasize that these tasks are predicated on models of the measurement, sampling, and nonresponse process whose assumptions cannot be fully tested. After describing this workflow in abstract terms, we then describe in detail how it can be applied to the analysis of historical and contemporary opinion polls. We also discuss extensions of the basic workflow, particularly inference for causal quantities and multilevel regression and poststratification.

**Keywords:** weighting, calibration, ecological inference, nonresponse, quota sampling



ISBNs: 9781108794152 (PB), 9781108879217 (OC)
ISSNs: 2398-4023 (online), 2514-3794 (print)

# Contents

## Introduction

This Element provides a concise overview of the use of adjustment weights to analyze unrepresentative survey samples. Such unrepresentativeness can arise from the process by which subjects are sampled from the population (e.g., if nonprobability sampling is used) or in the process by which survey responses are obtained from sampled subjects (e.g., if responses are nonrandomly missing). If related to outcome variables of interest, nonrandom sampling and/or nonresponse can bias estimators of population quantities. Almost all surveys, whether historical or contemporary, are at least somewhat vulnerable to such biases.

Adjustment weighting is a simple yet flexible method of addressing sampling and nonresponse bias. It entails assigning each sampled unit an adjustment weight, which is then incorporated into estimators. An advantage of weighting over alternative methods of adjustment, such as multiple imputation, is that it does not require an explicit parametric model for each outcome variable. Rather, adjustment weighting typically involves simple modifications of nonparametric design-based estimators for probability samples, which weight units by the inverse of their probability of being selected under the sampling design. This Element focuses on a framework for adjustment weighting known as calibration, which subsumes such commonly used methods as poststratification and raking. In this framework, a sample is "calibrated" to a set of population targets derived from auxiliary information (e.g., census data). Calibration ameliorates nonresponse bias to the extent that the variables that define these targets predict units' response probabilities and outcome values.

A distinguishing feature of this work is that we give equal weight (no pun intended) to two basic steps in the workflow of weighting-based survey inference: the estimation of population targets and the estimation of adjustment weights. The first step (target estimation), though typically ignored by texts on survey weighting, precedes the second step (weight estimation) temporally and can exceed it in complexity and difficulty. Auxiliary information often consists of partial, noisy, and internally inconsistent population estimates, and deriving a single set of population targets from this information is often far from straightforward. Like weight estimation, which requires good working models of the nonresponse mechanism and of the outcome of interest, target estimation implicitly depends on a measurement model relating the auxiliary information to the true population distribution.

In explaining the workflow of weighting-based survey inference, we employ a mix of theoretical discussion and empirical illustration. Section 1 sets the scene by emphasizing the ubiquity of sampling and nonresponse bias and explaining the problems this poses for classical design-based inference. It then describes in general terms how such biases can be ameliorated by incorporating auxiliary information into design-based estimators, and it outlines a general workflow for doing so. Section 2 delves into the specifics of adjustment weighting. It focuses on weight estimation, temporarily assuming that the auxiliary information is free from measurement error. It shows how calibration subsumes many commonly used weighting techniques and then discusses criteria and procedures for the critical task of selecting population targets. Relaxing the assumption of error-free auxiliary information, Section 3 turns to the typically neglected task of estimating population distributions and deriving population targets from them. Section 4 illustrates the tasks of calibration and target estimation in detail, using an application to a survey conducted before the 2016 US presidential election. Section 5 applies similar techniques to a more complex historical application: quota-sampled public opinion polls conducted between 1936 and 1952. Section 6 discusses methodological extensions and concludes. Key terms and abbreviations are defined in a glossary at the end of the Element.

To make it easier for readers to use the methods we describe, we provide illustrative code implementing them in the open-source statistical software R (R Core Team 2018). Each section ends with an appendix containing code snippets related to the topics discussed therein. In addition, all of the code in this Element can be accessed and run reproducibly on Code Ocean (`https://codeocean.com/`). There is a separate "capsule" for each section, all of which have the tag `caughey-et-al-weighting-element`. A direct link to each capsule can be found in the Example Code subsection of the corresponding section.

# 1 The Problem of Unrepresentative Survey Samples

## 1.1 Survey Sampling: From Quotas to Probability and Back Again

Opinion polling as we now know it originated in the mid-1930s with George Gallup's, Elmo Roper's, and Archibald Crossley's pioneering surveys of the American public (Converse 1987, 87). Unlike straw polls such as those conducted by *Literary Digest* magazine, which solicited survey responses from telephone directories and other class-biased lists, Gallup and his fellow pollsters consciously constructed samples that were relatively small but observably representative of the population of interest (in Gallup's case, the US electorate). They did so using the technique of **quota sampling**, in which interviewers were sent to purposively selected locations and instructed to interview specified proportions of subjects in distinct demographic categories (Berinsky 2006).

The accuracy of quota sampling was validated when these pollsters correctly predicted the outcome of the 1936 presidential election, a success which contrasted markedly with the failure of the much larger *Literary Digest* poll. The latter's poor performance was due to two compounding factors: the **sampling bias** caused by its unrepresentative sampling frame and the **nonresponse bias** caused by differential response rates, both of which skewed the *Literary Digest*'s sample in a Republican direction (Squire 1988). By forcing survey samples to match the target population in specified respects, quota sampling substantially reduced the scope for such biases.

Barely a decade later, however, quota sampling experienced its own embarrassing failure when Gallup and other pollsters mispredicted the 1948 presidential election.[1] Partly in response to this debacle, US survey organizations transitioned to a new procedure for selecting respondents: **probability sampling.**[2] Instead of constructing samples that match the target population in observable respects, probability sampling entails selecting interview subjects from the sampling frame at random according to known probabilities. By the 1950s, most commercial pollsters had adopted probability sampling, as had new academic survey organizations, such as the University of Michigan's **Survey Research Center (SRC)**.

Because almost all surveys continued to rely on in-person interviews, early probability samples were based on area sampling. By the 1970s, however, many commercial polling organizations had transitioned to telephone samples selected with **random digit dialing (RDD)**. Though issues of coverage error remained, probability sampling all but eliminated sampling bias in surveys. Moreover, survey response rates remained high, ranging from about 50% for the typical consumer telephone poll to more than 70% for academic surveys such as the **American National Election Studies (ANES)** and 95% for the best government surveys (Wiseman and McDonald 1979; Luevano 1994; Dixon and Tucker 2010, 597).

Since the 1980s, however, response rates for both in-person and telephone surveys have fallen dramatically, in the United States as well as in other countries (Leeuw and de Heer 2002). The response rate for the SRC's RDD-sampled

[1] According to a postmortem of election polling in 1948, this prediction failure actually had less to do with the deficiencies of quota sampling per se than with late opinion movement after the last polls were conducted (Mosteller et al. 1949).

[2] By the mid-1930s, Jerzy Neyman and other statisticians had laid the theoretical basis for probability sampling, and by the end of that decade area sampling methods were well established in the US Census Bureau and other government agencies. The practical merits of probability versus purposive sampling, however, continued to be debated for at least another decade (Berinsky 2006, 501–502).

Survey of Consumer Attitudes, for example, fell from about 70% in 1981 to just above 50% in 2006 (Dixon and Tucker 2010, 597). Face-to-face ANES surveys have followed a similar trajectory (Hillygus 2016). Declines among commercial telephone surveys have been even more precipitous. Response rates for Gallup surveys had dropped to 28% by 1997 and to 7% by 2017 (Marken 2018). Contemporary response rates for probability-based internet panels, which were developed in the 1990s, are if anything lower.

Given the theoretical potential for even a small amount of nonresponse to bias design-based survey estimators (Cochran 1977, 363; but see Groves 2006), these declines have seriously concerned pollsters and survey researchers. One reaction has been to rely more heavily on statistical methods for addressing nonresponse bias, including weighting (Brick and Montaquila 2009) and, less commonly, multiple imputation (Peytchev 2012). A more radical response has been to abandon probability sampling entirely and return to quota sampling, particularly for opt-in online panels (Ansolabehere and Rivers 2013) but also for telephone surveys (Moy 2015). Weighting, imputation, and quota sampling all require **auxiliary information** on the characteristics of the target population, which is available in increasing abundance (if not necessarily quality) from consumer databases, administrative records, and other sources. The importance of such adjustments was dramatically illustrated in 2016, when the undersampling of low-education white men contributed to election surveys' underestimation of Donald Trump's vote share in several key states (Kennedy et al. 2018).

Survey sampling has thus in a sense come full circle. Early opinion polls relied on quota sampling mainly because, in an age without widespread telephone access, it was the most cost-effective means of constructing approximately representative national samples. Despite lacking a firm basis in probability theory, quota samples seemed to work well enough in practice, at least by the metric of predicting election outcomes. The embarrassment of the 1948 election, in conjunction with the development of area-sampling methods, persuaded most American pollsters to switch to probability sampling. The advent of near-universal telephone access and development of RDD sampling, which was both probability-based and inexpensive, inaugurated what might be considered the golden age of survey sampling; but, like all golden ages, it was only temporary. By the twenty-first century, all but the highest-quality (and most-expensive) surveys suffered from response rates so low as to call into question the utility of solely design-based survey inference. Today, as in the 1930s, nearly all opinion surveys rely on purposive selection or adjustment (e.g., weighting) of their samples to render them observably representative of the population of interest.

## 1.2 Survey Inference with Unrepresentative Samples

As the foregoing overview suggests, for a fairly brief period it was plausible to draw population inferences from surveys based on their sampling design alone. When feasible, design-based statistical inference is straightforward and appealing, for it does not rely on hard-to-validate assumptions about the data-generating process for the survey outcome of interest. Nor does design-based inference require any auxiliary data beyond the sample itself (though incorporating auxiliary information can often increase estimators' precision). Rather, population means and other parameters can be consistently estimated based solely on knowledge of each population unit's **sampling probability** $\pi_i$.

### *1.2.1 Design-Based Inference without Auxiliary Information*

When the sampling model is known by design and all sampled individuals provide valid responses, the "workflow" of inference – the sequence of steps leading from population to sample to estimate – can proceed unproblematically along the bottom of Figure 1.1, without recourse to data beyond that contained in the sample itself. The circle in the lower left corner in this figure represents a target population $\mathcal{U}$ of $N$ units indexed by $i$. In this population, the outcome of interest $y$ and auxiliary variables $\boldsymbol{x}$ have the **joint distribution** $f_{\mathcal{U}}(y, \boldsymbol{x})$, and the target of inference is some parameter $\theta_y$ of $f_{\mathcal{U}}(y, \boldsymbol{x})$. To draw inferences about $\theta_y$, we rely on a sample $\mathcal{S}$ of size $n_{\mathcal{S}}$, of which a subset $\mathcal{R}$ of $n_{\mathcal{R}}$ responders (the **respondent set**) provide nonmissing responses with joint distribution $g_{\mathcal{R}}(y, \boldsymbol{x})$.[3] In a probability sample with full response, the sampling model that generated the observed data is known by design, and thus parameter estimation and inference can be based solely on that design.

In the case of a **simple random sample (SRS)**, where units' sampling probabilities $\pi_i$ are equal and independent across units, the sample average $\bar{y}_{\mathcal{S}} = n_{\mathcal{S}}^{-1} \sum_{i \in \mathcal{S}} y_i$ is an unbiased estimator of the population mean $\mu_y$. For more complex sampling designs in which the $\pi_i$, though known, are unequal and possibly correlated, unbiased estimation is provided by the **Horvitz-Thompson (HT)** estimator,

$$\hat{\mu}_y^{\mathrm{HT}} = \frac{\sum_{i \in \mathcal{S}} d_i y_i}{\mathrm{E}(\sum_{i \in \mathcal{S}} d_i)}, \tag{1.1}$$

[3] In this Element we consider only **unit nonresponse**, ignoring the possibility that a sampled unit might provide responses to some questions but not others (**item nonresponse**). For a useful discussion of methods for addressing item nonresponse, see Särndal and Lundstrom (2005, chap. 12).

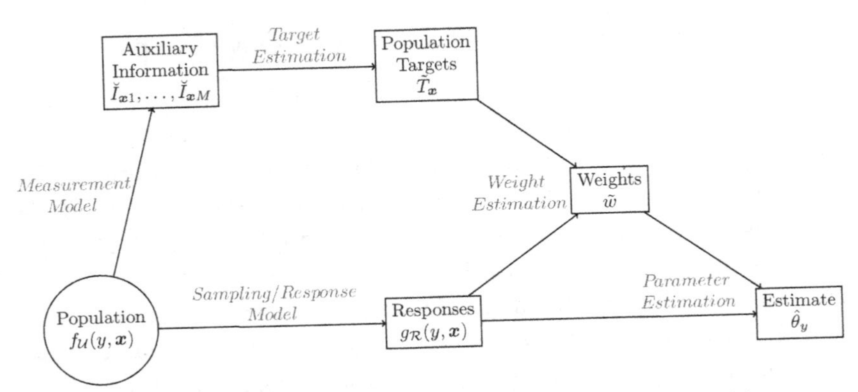


**Figure 1.1** The workflow of survey inference. Observed quantities are enclosed in rectangles and unobserved in circles. If the sampling model is fixed by design (i.e., the inclusion probabilities $\pi_i$ are known) and nonresponse is absent (i.e., $\rho_i = 1\ \forall i$), parameter estimation can proceed based on inverse-probability weights $d_i = 1/\pi_i$. In the face of unrepresentative sampling and/or nonresponse, however, weights must be calculated based on the population targets $\tilde{T}_{\boldsymbol{x}}$ and on assumptions about $\boldsymbol{x}$'s relationships with $\rho$ and $y$. The targets $\tilde{T}_{\boldsymbol{x}}$ themselves must be estimated based on auxiliary information $\breve{I}_{\boldsymbol{x}} = \{\breve{I}_{\boldsymbol{x}1}, \ldots, \breve{I}_{\boldsymbol{x}M}\}$ and a measurement model relating $f_{\mathcal{U}}(\boldsymbol{x})$ and $\breve{I}_{\boldsymbol{x}}$.

where $d_i = \pi_i^{-1}$ is $i$'s inverse probability or **design weight** and $\text{E}(\sum_{i \in \mathcal{S}} d_i)$ is the expected weighted sample size (Horvitz and Thompson 1952). Owing to the HT estimator's high variance, in practice it is often preferable to use the ratio or **Hájek estimator** of the mean,

$$\hat{\mu}_y^{\text{H}} = \frac{\sum_{i \in \mathcal{S}} d_i y_i}{\sum_{i \in \mathcal{S}} d_i}, \tag{1.2}$$

which substitutes the realized weighted sample size for the expected (Hájek 1958). Given probability sampling and full response, the Hájek estimator is consistent for $\mu_y$ and approximately unbiased,[4] and its sampling variance is generally substantially smaller than that of $\hat{\mu}_y^{\text{HT}}$ (Miratrix et al. 2018, 279; Aronow and Miller 2019, 228). Its approximate variance can be estimated as

$$\widehat{\text{var}}(\hat{\mu}_y^{\text{H}}) = \left(\sum_{i \in \mathcal{S}} d_i\right)^{-2} \sum_{i \in \mathcal{S}} \sum_{j \in \mathcal{S}} \frac{\pi_{ij} - \pi_i \pi_j}{\pi_{ij} \pi_i \pi_j} (y_i - \hat{\mu}_y^{\text{H}})(y_j - \hat{\mu}_y^{\text{H}}) \tag{1.3}$$

[4] Lumley (2010, 85) calls the ratio estimator "approximately unbiased" because its bias is much smaller than its standard error (proportional to $1/n$ rather than $1/\sqrt{n}$).

where $\pi_{ij}$ is the probability that both units $i$ and $j$ are sampled (Miratrix et al. 2018, appendix C). (For R code implementing the Hájek ratio estimator, see Listing 1.2.)

Alternatively, the sampling distribution of almost all common survey statistics, including $\hat{\mu}_y^{\text{H}}$, can be estimated via the **bootstrap**. A general procedure for bootstrapping complex sampling designs is to repeat the following $B$ times (e.g., $B = 999$):

1. Take a with-replacement sample of size $n_{\mathcal{S}}$ from $\mathcal{S}$, respecting the original sampling design (e.g., sampling each unit with probability proportional to $\pi_i$).
2. Using this bootstrap sample $\mathcal{S}^{(b)}$, calculate the estimate $\hat{\theta}_y^{(b)}$.

The resulting collection of bootstrap estimates $\{\hat{\theta}_y^{(1)}, \ldots, \hat{\theta}^{(B)}\}$ approximates the sampling distribution of $\hat{\theta}$. The standard deviation of the bootstrap distribution provides a consistent estimate of the standard error of the sampling distribution. Confidence intervals can also be estimated with the $\lfloor \alpha/2 \times B \rfloor^{\text{th}}$ and $\lceil (1-\alpha)/2 \times B \rceil^{\text{th}}$ largest values of the bootstrap distribution, where $1-\alpha$ is the level of the confidence interval (for the many variations and subtleties of the bootstrap, see Davison and Hinkley 1997). The bootstrap is thus a valuable alternative when analytical formulas for sampling distributions are unknown or unreliable. (For R code implementing the bootstrap, see Listings 1.1 and 1.2.)

Unfortunately, most real-world surveys do not approximate the ideal conditions required for design-based inference. Even high-quality probability-sampled surveys, in which $\pi_i$ is known for each unit, usually do not obtain valid responses from every sampled individual. In such cases, the respondent set $\mathcal{R}$ is a proper subset of the sample $\mathcal{S}$. Moreover, units' ex ante probability of responding if sampled (their **response probability** $\rho_i$) is typically both unknown and heterogeneous across units. Under such conditions, the consistency of design-based estimators is no longer guaranteed. In an SRS with nonresponse, for example, the bias of the unweighted sample mean is

$$\text{E}(\bar{y}) - \mu_y = R_{\rho y}\sigma_\rho\sigma_y/\bar{\rho}, \qquad (1.4)$$

where $R_{\rho y}$ is the population correlation between $\rho$ and $y$, $\sigma_\rho$ and $\sigma_y$ are the population standard deviations of $\rho$ and $y$, and $\bar{\rho}$ is the population average of $\rho$ (Bethlehem, Cobben, and Schouten 2011, 249). The bias of the HT estimator has a similar form that also depends on the association between $\rho$ and $y$ (Bethlehem 1988). In short, unless the outcome of interest is independent of population units' probabilities of being sampled and responding, purely design-based estimators will in general be biased and inconsistent.

### 1.2.2 Adjustment Weighting to Address Sampling and Nonresponse Bias

The most common method for addressing bias due to unrepresentative sampling and nonresponse is **adjustment weighting**, which includes common techniques such as **poststratification** and **raking** as well as the more general framework of **calibration** (Deville and Särndal 1992). Unlike design weights, which can be derived from the sampling design before the survey has been conducted, **adjustment weights** must be calculated afterwards based on the data actually obtained. Adjustment weights are, however, analogous to design weights in that they can be incorporated into estimators of population parameters. The weighting estimator for the mean, for example, has the same form as the Hájek estimator in (1.2) but with the adjustment weights $\tilde{w}_i$ substituted for the design-based ones $d_i$:

$$\hat{\mu}_y^{\mathrm{W}} = \frac{\sum_{i \in \mathcal{R}} \tilde{w}_i y_i}{\sum_{i \in \mathcal{R}} \tilde{w}_i}. \tag{1.5}$$

Unlike $d_i$, $\tilde{w}_i$ is a random quantity whose value must be calculated from auxiliary data beyond that contained in the sample itself. Specifically, calculating $\tilde{w}$ requires **population targets** $\tilde{T}_{\boldsymbol{x}} = \{\tilde{T}_{\boldsymbol{x}1}, \ldots, \tilde{T}_{\boldsymbol{x}G}\}$ for certain **auxiliary variables** $\boldsymbol{x}$ measured in the survey. Suppose, for example, that we wished to weight an SRS of adults to match the proportion of men and women in the population (a simple example of poststratification). In this case, two-category gender would be the only auxiliary variable, and the population targets would consist of estimates of the proportion of men and women in the population, $\tilde{T}_{\boldsymbol{x}} = (\tilde{P}_{\text{men}}, \tilde{P}_{\text{women}})$, derived from auxiliary information $\breve{I}_{\boldsymbol{x}}$ external to the sample itself. Each male respondent would be assigned the weight

$$\tilde{w}_i = \tilde{P}_{\text{men}} / p_{\text{men}}, \tag{1.6}$$

where $p_{\text{men}}$ is the proportion male among respondents. Weights for women would be defined analogously. Because each gender's weight would be proportional to its underrepresentation in the respondent set relative to the population, this adjustment would ensure that the weighted respondent set matched the gender breakdown in the population.

Weighting eliminates nonresponse bias if it renders the response probability $\rho$ and the outcome $y$ totally uncorrelated, as is the case in an SRS with full response. In principle, this condition can be satisfied if, conditional on the auxiliary variables $\boldsymbol{x}$, survey responses are either (1) **missing at random (MAR)** or (2) **independent and identically distributed (IID)**. For example, in the case of poststratification, bias is eliminated if either (1) $\rho$ is constant within cells or

(2) $y$ is IID within cells. In practice, adjustment weighting is unlikely to exactly satisfy either of these conditions, but substantial reductions in nonresponse bias are nevertheless possible if $\boldsymbol{x}$ strongly predicts both $\rho$ and $y$.

Because the beneficial effects of weighting can depend heavily on which auxiliary variables are available and on the specific outcome of interest, applied methodological texts typically recommend that auxiliary variables be selected with great care (e.g., Särndal and Lundstrom 2005; Lumley 2010; Bethlehem, Cobben, and Schouten 2011). Given that there may be multiple outcomes of interest in a given survey, it can even be desirable to use different sets of weights for different analyses of the same survey data. Few texts, however, provide much concrete guidance on how exactly to select auxiliary variables. Perhaps for this reason, the overwhelming majority of applied survey researchers seem instead to rely on only a single set of weights – often ones provided by the original creators of the dataset they are analyzing. Such reliance on a single set of (design) weights may be reasonable when analyzing probability samples with minimal nonresponse, but it is less tenable if units' probability of being sampled or of responding are not known ex ante.

### 1.2.3 Constructing Population Targets from Auxiliary Data

While the selection of auxiliary variables may be neglected, survey methodologists (not to mention practitioners) have given even less attention to the construction of the population targets used to create the weights in the first place.[5] In poststratification, for example, it is almost universally assumed that the cell population proportions $\tilde{P}_c$ are known exactly rather than estimated. More generally, survey researchers generally presume that they possess a direct measure of $f_{\mathcal{U}}(\boldsymbol{x})$, the joint distribution of auxiliary variables in the population. This presumption is frequently unjustified. Rather, the auxiliary information $\breve{I}_{\boldsymbol{x}}$ to which researchers have access often consists of $M$ disparate,

[5] We are not aware of any textbook on survey weighting that gives more than cursory attention to target estimation, though Valliant, Dever, and Kreuter (2018) do offer a brief discussion. The following quotation, from Gelman (2007, 155), while unusual for explicitly acknowledging that population targets must be estimated, nevertheless indicates the general neglect of this problem:

> In some cases the cell populations are unknown and must be estimated. For example, [in] the Current Population Survey . . . the counts are too sparse to directly estimate deep interactions (e.g., the proportion who are white females, 30–45, married, with less than a high school education, etc.) . . . For this paper, we shall ignore this difficulty and treat the [cell counts] as known.

noisy, and possibly inconsistent data sources, $\{\breve{I}_{x1}, \ldots, \breve{I}_{xM}\}$, from which estimated population targets $\tilde{T}_x$ must be derived (Deville 2000; Caughey and Wang 2019).

To illustrate, consider the relatively favorable scenario where a government census has collected data on all possible auxiliary variables. In the United States, privacy concerns preclude the release of the full individual-level census files for many decades after the Census is conducted. Fortunately, individual-level census data are available in the form of 1% or 5% microsamples, though to avoid identifying individual respondents the microdata sometimes mask certain variables, such as urban residence (see, e.g., Ruggles et al. 2017). However, the US Census Bureau often separately reports the aggregate distribution of the masked variables, sometimes cross-classified with other demographic or geographic factors such as race or state. The Census also conducts special surveys, such as the **Current Population Study (CPS)**, that contain more or less accurate estimates of other variables, such as self-reported voter turnout. As a final complication, these various data sources are typically available at irregular intervals – once per decade in the case of the full US Census, annually in the case of the CPS, and sometimes in between in the case of aggregate data such as urban residence.

Population estimates derived from such disparate sources of auxiliary information are subject to several sources of error and other complications. The first is simply random sampling error. The confidence interval for a percentage estimated from the 60,000-observation CPS, for example, can have a width of nearly a percentage point.[6] Even the sampling variability of census microsamples, which typically contain at least 1 million observations, can be nontrivial for some purposes, such as estimation at the level of states or other subpopulations. Only aggregate data that summarize the entire universe of cases, such as census reports on urban population by state, are entirely free of sampling error.

A second, potentially more serious source of error stems from systematic mismeasurement (or differential measurement) of auxiliary variables in the population or the sample. Not only does self-reported turnout, for instance, tend to be exaggerated by survey respondents but the magnitude of overreporting varies systematically across population groups (Ansolabehere and Hersh 2012). It may therefore be problematic to treat the CPS as an unbiased estimate of the voting population.[7] To take an example we consider in more detail

6 For example, the width of the 95% confidence interval for an estimated percentage of 50% is $\sqrt{0.5 \times (1 - 0.5)/60{,}000} \times 1.96 \times 2 = 0.8\%$.

7 Although the CPS is a very high-quality survey, scholars have shown that its estimates of turnout and other quantities still suffer from nontrivial bias and have devised weights to address this problem (e.g., Hur and Achen 2013; McDonald 2019).

in Section discussion of early public opinion polls, an auxiliary variable such as phone ownership may be operationalized differently in the survey and the auxiliary information (e.g., with respect to how telephones shared between two residences are coded).

The sparse and irregular structure of auxiliary data sources presents further challenges. The fact that the US Census is conducted every ten years forces analysts to interpolate and/or extrapolate into noncensus years – whether implicitly by treating targets as static or explicitly with a model of demographic change. The irregular and inconsistent structure of different data sources presents even greater difficulties. The fact that urban residence is not included in the census microdata, for example, means that its joint distribution with other census variables is not known – only its marginal distribution is (from aggregate US Census reports). As a result, urban residence cannot be used to define cells for poststratification, and either urban must be dropped as an auxiliary variable or an alternative weighting method, such as raking, must be used.

In short, it is frequently impossible to transform auxiliary information directly into population targets for use in weighting. This presents survey researchers with difficult choices. In many cases, they must drop auxiliary variables, abandon their preferred weighting method, and/or rely on modeling assumptions to construct an adequate estimate of the population targets $\tilde{T}_x$. Despite the importance of these choices, they have been given extremely little attention. Indeed, methodological texts on survey weighting almost always present population targets as given, hardly mentioning the possibility that targets might be error-prone or difficult to construct. By contrast, this text treats the construction of population targets as an integral part of the weighting process and accordingly discusses it at length in Section 3.

### 1.2.4 The Workflow of Weighting-Based Survey Inference

If a survey sample has been collected with nonprobability methods or is afflicted with substantial nonresponse, inference can rarely be based on design alone, and the statistical workflow cannot proceed directly along the bottom of Figure 1.1. Rather, inference must be at least partly model-based, and the workflow must involve several additional steps, represented by the "detour" along the top of Figure 1.1.

Beginning in the lower-right corner of Figure 1.1 and working backward, the first additional step is the incorporation of adjustment weights $\tilde{w}$ into estimators of parameters of interest. Unlike the design weights $d$, which can be derived from the sampling design alone, $\tilde{w}$ must be estimated using externally derived population targets, $\tilde{T}_x$. In simple cases, the relevant population targets (e.g., for poststratification by gender, the proportion of males and females in the population) may be known essentially without error. More typically, however, $\tilde{T}_x$ must itself be estimated from one or more sources of auxiliary information, $\breve{I}_x = \{\breve{I}_{x1}, \ldots, \breve{I}_{xM}\}$.

The workflow of weighting-based survey inference ultimately relies on two broad sets of modeling assumptions, represented by the two arrows emanating from the Population node in Figure 1.1. The first, which also undergirds design-based inference, is the "Sampling/Response Model," a set of assumptions about the process by which units were sampled from the population and their survey responses were obtained. Even design-based inference relies at least implicitly on modeling assumptions that cannot fully be verified. "In practice," notes Deville (1991, 176), "sampling for a probabilistic survey is a model to which the reality of data collection attempts to conform." The necessity of such a model, however, is particularly obvious for nonprobability samples and for surveys with substantial nonresponse. In either case, drawing population inferences from the observed sample requires assumptions about how subjects were sampled, why they decided to respond, and the observed variables that explain the sampling and response processes.

The second set of modeling assumptions, which we label the "Measurement Model," concern the relationship between the auxiliary information $\breve{I}_x$ and the population distribution $f_{\mathcal{U}}(\boldsymbol{x})$. Rarely can $\breve{I}_x$ be taken as a direct measure of $f_{\mathcal{U}}(\boldsymbol{x})$. Even the simple case of census microdata, in which $\breve{I}_x$ may be a random sample from $f_{\mathcal{U}}(\boldsymbol{x})$, requires assumptions about the definition of the target population, the measurement of auxiliary variables, and the process by which individual census records were sampled. A more elaborate measurement model is required if the auxiliary information is measured at a different point in time than the survey or if its data structure differs from that required for the weighting targets (e.g., if $\breve{I}_x$ consists of separate marginal distributions rather than the full joint distribution). Assumptions about all of these aspects of the measurement process are required to translate the auxiliary information into usable population targets.

Design-based inference is a limiting case in which sampling and response probabilities are assumed to be known, thus obviating the need for auxiliary information. Another simple case is poststratification, which assumes that nonresponse is MAR within strata whose population proportions are known. In many cases, such simple sampling and measurement models are often untenable: the sampling procedure is less than fully random, the nonresponse mechanism is unknown, and the auxiliary information does not exactly match the requirements of the weighting procedure. Inference must therefore proceed on the basis of more complicated and debatable assumptions. In such contexts, it is unrealistic to expect perfectly unbiased estimation of population quantities. The solution, however, is not to retreat to design-based estimators whose assumptions are clearly violated but to base inference on defensible sampling and measurement models, with the aim of reducing bias if not eliminating it.

## 1.3 Example Code

The Code Ocean capsule for this section is published at `https://doi.org/10.24433/CO.9047395.v1`.

Listing 1.1 Load data and create survey objects

```
1  ## Libraries
2  library(survey)     # for analyzing complex surveys (see Lumley 2010)
3
4  # LOAD DATA AND CREATE SURVEY DESIGN OBJECTS
5
6  ## Read data
7  gss_df <- readRDS("data/GSS2016_use.rds") # survey data
8  acs_df <- readRDS("data/ACS2016_use.rds") # auxiliary information
9
10 ## Create design-weighted svydesign objects
11 gss_dwt <- svydesign(ids = ~vpsu, weights = ~design_wt, strata = ~vstrat,
12                      data = gss_df, nest = TRUE)
13 acs_dwt <- svydesign(ids = ~1, weight = ~perwt, data = acs_df)
```

Listing 1.2 Inference for various population quantities

```
1  ## Proportion male
2  svymean(~male, design = gss_dwt) # males underrepresented in sample
3
4  ## Proportion black among males
5  svymean(~black, design = subset(gss_dwt, male == 1))
6  svyratio(~I(male*black), ~male, gss_dwt) # same because the mean is a ratio
7
8  ## Mean and quantiles of age (integer-valued)
9  svymean(~age_int, gss_dwt, na.rm = TRUE)                              # analytic SE
10 svymean(~age_int, gss_boot, na.rm = TRUE)                             # bootstrp SE
11 svyquantile(~age_int, gss_dwt, q = seq(.1, .9, .1), na.rm = TRUE)   # no SE
12 svyquantile(~age_int, gss_boot, q = seq(.1, .9, .1), na.rm = TRUE)  # bootstrp SE
```

# 2 Weight Estimation

This section discusses **weight estimation**: the process of deriving adjustment weights $\tilde{w}$ from population targets $\tilde{T}_{\boldsymbol{x}}$ for use in parameter estimation. For the sake of this discussion, we temporarily assume that the auxiliary information $\breve{I}_{\boldsymbol{x}}$ consists of the **joint distribution** of the auxiliary variables $\boldsymbol{x}$ and is measured without error. That is, we assume for now that $\breve{I}_{\boldsymbol{x}} = f_{\mathcal{U}}(\boldsymbol{x})$. (This assumption is relaxed in Section 3, which covers **target estimation**.) We first introduce two well-known weighting methods, poststratification and raking, and then show

how they can be subsumed into the more general framework of calibration estimation. We then turn to the issue of choosing among weighting methods, which in the calibration framework reduces to two decisions: the choice of population targets $\tilde{T}_{\boldsymbol{x}}$ and, much less important, the choice of how to measure the discrepancy between the design weights $d$ and the adjustment weights $\tilde{w}$. We stress the importance of selecting population targets for variables that strongly predict both nonresponse and the outcome of interest. We discuss methods for partially automating the choice of population targets but caution that purely statistical criteria for target selection should be balanced against substantive knowledge and interpretability.

## 2.1 Common Weighting Methods

### *2.1.1 Poststratification*

The two most common forms of survey weighting are poststratification and raking. **Poststratification** entails classifying the population into $C$ mutually exclusive and exhaustive strata ("cells") and assigning responding units weights that ensure that the weighted proportion of sampled units in every cell $c$ matches $c$'s proportion of the population. Typically, though not necessarily, cells are defined by a complete cross-classification of multiple auxiliary variables (e.g., gender, race, and state of residence). The population targets required for poststratification are thus $\tilde{T}_{\boldsymbol{x}} = \{\tilde{P}_1, \ldots, \tilde{P}_C\}$, where $\boldsymbol{x}$ denotes the auxiliary variables that define the cells and $\tilde{P}_c$ denotes the target proportion for cell $c$.

The special case of poststratification weights for a **simple random sample (SRS)** was illustrated in (1.6). In the general case where units differ in their sampling probabilities, the formula is

$$\tilde{w}_i^{\text{PS}} = (\tilde{P}_{c[i]}/\hat{P}^{\text{H}}_{c[i]}) \times d_i, \tag{2.1}$$

where $c[i]$ denotes the cell $c$ that contains $i$ and $\hat{P}^{\text{H}}_{c[i]}$ is the Hájek estimator of cell $c$'s population proportion (see Listing 2.3).[8] The weights in (2.1) force the weighted group size of each cell $c$ to exactly equal $\tilde{P}_c$.[9] As was noted in Section 1.2.2, the poststratification estimator of the population mean,

$$\hat{\mu}_y^{\text{PS}} = \frac{\sum_{i \in \mathcal{R}} \tilde{w}_i^{\text{PS}} y_i}{\sum_{i \in \mathcal{R}} \tilde{w}_i^{\text{PS}}}, \tag{2.2}$$

[8] That is, $\hat{P}^{\text{H}}_{c[i]} = \sum_{i \in \mathcal{R}} d_i 1_{i \in c} / \sum_{i \in \mathcal{R}} d_i$ is the design-weighted proportion of cell $c$ in the respondent set.

[9] Note that in contrast to (1.6), which gives poststratification weights for an SRS, the weights in (2.1) may vary within cells because they depend on the design weights $d_i$.

is consistent and approximately unbiased if $y$ and $\rho$ are uncorrelated within cells.[10] Analytic formulas for estimating the sampling variance of poststratification and other weighting estimators are available (see, e.g., Särndal and Lundstrom 2005; Kott 2006), but a general alternative is to estimate the sampling distribution with the **bootstrap** (Section 1.2.1), making sure to recalculate the weights $\tilde{w}_i^{\text{PS}}$ in each bootstrap sample (see Listing 2.5).

### *2.1.2 Raking*

If the cells are defined by a cross-classification of auxiliary variables $\boldsymbol{x}$, poststratification requires population targets for the joint distribution of those variables, $f_{\mathcal{U}}(\boldsymbol{x})$. By contrast, **raking** requires only their **marginal distributions**. Suppose, for example, that $\boldsymbol{x}$ consisted of three categorical variables: *gender* (male/female), *race* (black/white/other), and *state*. Poststratification on these variables would require the population proportion of each gender-race-state group, for a total of $2 \times 3 \times 50 = 300$ population targets. Raking, however, would require only the proportions of each gender, race, and state, respectively, or $2 + 3 + 50 = 55$ targets. Poststratification ensures that the weighted sample matches the auxiliary variables' joint distribution in the population, whereas raking matches only their marginal distributions.[11]

Given that poststratification forces a closer match between sample and population, why would raking be used? One reason is that poststratification requires more detailed auxiliary information, which may not be available. If only marginal population targets are available, then raking (or something similar) may be the only feasible weighting method. Another barrier to poststratification is the presence of empty population cells in the sample. If such cells exist, then either some cells must be merged or an alternative method such as raking must be used. Even when poststratification is feasible, raking may still be preferable if the cell sizes are small, which can result in large within-sample variation in cell weights and thus high-variance estimators. From the perspective of **mean squared error (MSE)**, the greater efficiency of raking may well be worth a small increase in bias.

Under what conditions does raking lead to minimal increase in bias relative to poststratification on the same set of auxiliary variables? When the effects of

---

[10] Its "approximate" unbiasedness stems from the fact that in a non-SRS probability sample the ratio estimate $\hat{P}^{\text{H}}_{c[i]}$ in (2.1) has a small finite-sample bias (see footnote 4). This approximation can be eliminated by substituting the (more variable) Horvitz-Thompson estimate $\hat{P}^{\text{HT}}_{c[i]}$.

[11] Unlike poststratification weights, there is no analytic formula for raking weights, but the latter can be calculated using a procedure known as iterative proportional fitting, which involves iteratively adjusting the design weights to match each margin in succession until the weights stabilize (Deming and Stephan 1940).

the auxiliary variables are, in a certain sense, additive rather than interactive. In particular, raking is justified under a model in which the inverse of each unit's response probability (its **response influence** $\omega_i \equiv \rho_i^{-1}$) is a log-linear additive function of the auxiliary variables. The response influence can be thought of as the unobserved counterpart of the observed design weight $d_i \equiv \pi_i^{-1}$. Under a log-linear model for $\omega_i$, raking yields weights $\tilde{w}_i^{\text{rake}}$ that are consistent estimates of $\omega_i d_i$, and thus in turn produces consistent weighting estimators of population quantities such as $\mu_y$ (Binder and Théberge 1988).

To illustrate, consider the case of an SRS with two auxiliary variables, gender and race, whose combinations result in $2 \times 3 = 6$ cells (for a similar example, see Little and Wu 1991). If a log-linear model holds, then the expected response influence of each unit $i$ with gender $g$ and race $r$ is

$$\mathrm{E}(\omega_{g[i]r[i]}) = \mathrm{e}^{\lambda_0 + \alpha_{g[i]} + \beta_{r[i]}}, \tag{2.3}$$

where $\alpha_g$ is the effect of gender $g$ and $\beta_r$ the effect of race $r$. Raking to match the population margins of gender and race yields weights of the form

$$\tilde{w}_{g[i]r[i]}^{\text{rake}} = \mathrm{e}^{\hat{\lambda}_0 + \hat{\alpha}_{g[i]} + \hat{\beta}_{r[i]}}, \tag{2.4}$$

where $\hat{\lambda}_0$, $\hat{\alpha}_{g[i]}$, and $\hat{\beta}_{r[i]}$ solve the constraints imposed by the marginal targets. These weights, which are constant within cells, imply the following set of population targets for the cell proportions:

$$\tilde{P}_{gr}^{\text{rake}} = p_{gr}\mathrm{e}^{\hat{\lambda}_0 + \hat{\alpha}_{g[i]} + \hat{\beta}_{r[i]}}, \tag{2.5}$$

where $p_{gr}$ is the proportion of the sample with gender $g$ and race $r$.[12] Under the log-linear model in (2.3), $\tilde{P}_{gr}^{\text{rake}}$ is the maximum likelihood estimate of the population cell proportion $P_{gr}$ (Little and Wu 1991, 88).

As these implied population targets suggest, raking can be thought of a variant of poststratification in which the actual cell proportions $\tilde{\mathbf{P}}^{\text{PS}}$ are replaced with the estimated cell targets $\tilde{\mathbf{P}}^{\text{rake}}$ (Little 1993, 1010). In other words, raking is equivalent to poststratifying the sample to the "smoothed" cell targets $\tilde{\mathbf{P}}^{\text{rake}}$, which are equal to the sample proportions $p_{gr}$ times an adjustment to which each variable contributes independently (that is, additively on the log scale). If the log-linear model is true, then raking targets $\tilde{\mathbf{P}}^{\text{rake}}$ will have the same expectation as the corresponding poststratification targets $\tilde{\mathbf{P}}^{\text{PS}}$, but will have lower sampling variability.

[12] In a non-SRS probability sample, $p_{gr}$ would be replaced with the design-weighted estimate of the proportion, $\hat{P}_{gr}^{\text{H}}$.

## 2.2 Calibration

Both poststratification and raking can be subsumed under a more general framework known as **calibration** (Deville and Särndal 1992). In this framework, a sample is "calibrated" to the population by calculating weights that ensure that the weighted sample exactly matches a set of population targets $\tilde{T}_{\boldsymbol{x}}$. The goal of calibration is to find the vector of weights $\tilde{w}$ that differ as little as possible from the design weights $d$ while also matching the targets.

Formally, calibration finds the set of weights $\tilde{w}$ that, for some distance measure $D(\cdot,\cdot)$, minimizes the sum

$$\sum_{i\in\mathcal{R}} D(\tilde{w}_i, d_i) \tag{2.6}$$

subject to the $K$ constraints

$$\tilde{T}_{\boldsymbol{x}k} = \sum_{i\in\mathcal{R}} \tilde{w}_i z_{ik},\ k \in 1\ldots K, \tag{2.7}$$

where each element of the **auxiliary vector** $\boldsymbol{z}_i$ is a function of the auxiliary variables $\boldsymbol{x}_i$. For example, in the case of calibration on the indicator variable *urban* ($x_i \in \{0,1\}$), we have $K = 1$, $z_{ik} = x_i$, and $\tilde{T}_{\boldsymbol{x}} = \tilde{\mu}_x$ (the urban proportion of the population). More generally, $\boldsymbol{z}_i$ can consist of a set of indicators for the levels of a single categorical $x_i$ (as in one-way poststratification), for the levels of multiple auxiliary variables (as in raking), or for the cross-classification of multiple variables (as in multi-way poststratification). Moreover, since calibration does not require that the auxiliary variables be categorical, $z_{ik}$ can also be some continuous transformation of one or more auxiliary variable. Thus, for example, a sample could be calibrated to the first and second moments of the age distribution in the population by using the auxiliary vector $\boldsymbol{z}_i = (age_i,\ age_i^2)$. Although it is not always possible to satisfy these constraints – no set of weights can compensate for an empty cell in the sample, for example – when calibration is feasible, the weighted sample will exactly match the population moments specified in $\tilde{T}_{\boldsymbol{x}}$.

In the calibration framework, different weighting methods are distinguished by their distance measure $D(\cdot,\cdot)$ and the form of the targets $\tilde{T}_{\boldsymbol{x}}$. Poststratification (a form of **linear weighting**) uses the distance measure $D^{\chi^2}(\tilde{w}_i, d_i) = (\tilde{w}_i - d_i)^2/d_i$ and calibrates to the population totals for a mutually exclusive and exhaustive set of cells. In contrast, raking (a form of **entropy weighting**) uses the entropy distance $D^{\text{ent}}(\tilde{w}_i, d_i) = w_i \log(w_i/d_i)$ and calibrates to the marginal totals of the auxiliary variables.[13] Other distance measures, such as that used by "logit" calibration, are also possible (Deville and Särndal 1992).

Although calibration weights can vary slightly depending on what distance measure is used, the differences are typically small (see Listings 2.4; see also Kalton and Flores-Cervantes 2003, 85, table 2). Different distance metrics do have their respective advantages. Linear weighting is analytically and computationally tractable, entropy weighting guarantees positive weights, and logit calibration places upper and lower bounds on the weights. In general, however, the choice of distance metric is typically much less important than the choice of population targets (Lumley 2010, 166).

## 2.3 Criteria for Auxiliary Vectors

The overriding importance of the choice of population targets $\tilde{T}_{\boldsymbol{x}}$ – and thus of the auxiliary vector $\boldsymbol{z}$ – can be seen more clearly by examining the formula for the "nearbias" of the calibration estimator $\hat{\mu}_y^{\mathrm{W}}$. (The exact bias depends on an additional term that tends to zero as the sample sizes grows, but the nearbias provides a close approximation even in modest samples.) The nearbias of $\hat{\mu}_y^{\mathrm{W}}$ is given by the expression

$$\text{nearbias}(\hat{\mu}_y^{\mathrm{W}}) = -N^{-1} \sum_{i \in \mathcal{U}} (1 - \rho_i) e_{\rho i}, \tag{2.8}$$

where $e_{\rho i} \equiv y_i - \boldsymbol{z}_i' \boldsymbol{B}_{\mathcal{U};\rho}$ is $i$'s residual from the $\rho$-weighted population regression of $y$ on $\boldsymbol{z}$ (Särndal and Lundstrom 2005, 98–99).

This formula highlights several important features of the bias of $\hat{\mu}_y^{\mathrm{W}}$. Consistent with the asymptotic equivalence of different weighting methods noted by Little and Wu (1991, 88), the nearbias does *not* depend on choice of the distance measure $D(\cdot, \cdot)$ but rather on the choice of auxiliary vector $\boldsymbol{z}_i$. Specifically, the nearbias depends on the correlation between $y$ and $\rho$ conditional on $\boldsymbol{z}_i$. One way this correlation can be broken is if the residuals $e$ from an unweighted population regression of $y$ on $\boldsymbol{z}$ are uncorrelated with $\rho$. This includes the special case where the outcome is perfectly predicted by a linear combination of the auxiliary vector (i.e., $y_i = \boldsymbol{\beta}' \boldsymbol{z}_i \; \forall i \in \mathcal{U}$, for some vector $\boldsymbol{\beta}$), in which case $e_i = 0 \; \forall i$. The nearbias is also eliminated if the auxiliary vector linearly predicts the response influence (i.e., $\omega_i = \boldsymbol{\lambda}' \boldsymbol{z}_i \; \forall i \in \mathcal{U}$, for some vector $\boldsymbol{\lambda}$).[14] The latter condition includes the special cases of full response ($\rho_i = 1 \; \forall i \in \mathcal{U}$) and uniform response probabilities ($\rho_i = \rho \; \forall i \in \mathcal{U}$) (Särndal and Lundstrom 2005, 101–102).

[13] Ireland and Kullback (1968). For a causal inference perspective on entropy weighting, see Hainmueller (2012).

[14] This holds under the condition that at least one element of $\boldsymbol{z}_i$ is nonzero for all population units.

In actual surveys, none of the above conditions is likely to be satisfied exactly. Nevertheless, the theoretical conditions for zero nearbias illustrate the most important criteria for selecting the auxiliary vector $\boldsymbol{z}$. Specifically, as Särndal and Lundstrom (2005, 22) note, the ideal auxiliary vector should

1. strongly predict the outcome of interest $y$;
2. strongly predict the probability of responding $\rho$; and
3. identify the domains (subpopulations) of interest.

The third criterion can be thought of as a specific restatement of the general maxim to calibrate weights to the population of interest – in this case, a subset of a larger population. So, for example, if the parameters of interest are the mean ages of men and of women, then the population targets should be broken down by gender (i.e., each auxiliary variable should be interacted with gender).

Adjustment weighting is sometimes described as entailing a bias-variance trade-off, but this is not necessarily true (Little and Vartivarian 2005). In the presence of nonresponse, an auxiliary vector that strongly predicts both the outcome of interest $y$ and the probability of response $\rho$ will generally reduce a calibration estimator's variance as well as its bias. However, an auxiliary vector with a robust association with $\rho$ but a weak one with $y$ will increase variance without substantially reducing bias. Conversely, a strong association with $y$ but a weak one with $\rho$ reduces variance without much of an effect on bias. Although the ideal $\boldsymbol{z}$ would predict both $y$ and $\rho$, these effects would seem to argue for prioritizing the former over the latter. The disadvantage of doing so, however, is that it requires a different auxiliary vector (and thus a different set of weights) for each outcome variable, whereas prioritizing the prediction of $\rho$ does not. Again, though: $\boldsymbol{z}$ must be at least somewhat predictive of each outcome of interest or else weighting will increase variance without reducing bias.

## 2.4 Selecting an Auxiliary Vector

How exactly should analysts select an auxiliary vector that maximizes the criteria stated in Section 2.3? To some degree, the selection problem can be automated. Särndal and Lundstrom (2008), for example, recommend an $R^2$-like statistic that captures variability in predicted response probabilities and propose that it be used in a stepwise selection procedure for the "best possible" auxiliary vector. Owing to the computational burden, however, Särndal and Lundstrom restrict their attention to "main effects" only – that is, to the marginal rather than joint distributions of the auxiliary variables. Wagner (2012) surveys a wider array of nonresponse indicators, including some that take into account auxiliary vectors' relationship with outcome variables, but does not propose a procedure for using them to select an auxiliary vector. Others, such as Andridge and Little (2011), do propose such procedures but focus on maximum-likelihood or other model-based estimators.

Recently, Caughey and Hartman (2017) have proposed framing the choice of auxiliary vector as a variable-selection problem. If nonresponse bias is reduced to the extent that the conditions $y_i = \boldsymbol{\lambda}'\boldsymbol{z}_i \; \forall i \in \mathcal{U}$ and $\omega_i = \boldsymbol{\lambda}'\boldsymbol{z}_i \; \forall i \in \mathcal{U}$ are satisfied, then the goal should be to select the $\boldsymbol{z}_i^*$ that best predicts both $y_i$ and $\omega_i$. Unless the set of auxiliary variables $\boldsymbol{x}$ is small, it is not computationally feasible to search over the set of possible auxiliary vectors and select the one with the highest $R^2$ (or other fit criterion). Caughey and Hartman thus suggest the use of the least absolute shrinkage and selection operator, or lasso (Tibshirani 1996), as a computationally efficient means of selecting the optimal $\boldsymbol{z}_i^*$. They propose an algorithm whose starting point is a (multivariate) regression of $y_i$ and/or an estimate of $\omega_i$ on a high-order interaction of the auxiliary variables $\boldsymbol{x}$. The algorithm begins with a low complexity penalty, but the penalty is successively increased until a $\boldsymbol{z}_i^*$ is found for which calibration is possible.[15]

The best auxiliary vector is not necessarily the most complex one for which calibration is feasible. Usually, the more complex the vector, the greater the variation in weights, which in turn can increase estimators' variance. One common indicator of variance inflation is Kish's (1965) **design effect due to weighting,**

$$\text{deff}_{\text{Kish}} = 1 + \text{var}(\tilde{w})/\bar{\tilde{w}}^2, \tag{2.9}$$

where $\text{var}(\tilde{w})$ and $\bar{\tilde{w}}$ are, respectively, the sample variance and mean of the weights. Under certain assumptions (notably, probability sampling and homoskedasticity of $y$), $\text{deff}_{\text{Kish}}$ measures the ratio of the sampling variance of $\hat{\mu}_y$ with unequal weights relative to its variance with equal ones. A common rule of thumb is to limit weight variability (by coarsening the auxiliary vector or trimming extreme weights)[16] if $\text{deff}_{\text{Kish}} > 1.5$, under the logic that any increase in bias from doing so will be more than counterbalanced by a decrease in variance. As Valliant, Dever, and Kreuter (2018, 395–414) note, however, such ad hoc procedures lack firm theoretical grounding. Moreover, under certain conditions (e.g., when nonresponse is substantial) large variation in weights can actually be conducive to efficient estimation. We therefore caution against any automatic rule for limiting weight variability: it should be done only when there is affirmative reason to believe that extreme weights are increasing variance without a compensating decrease in bias.

15 The more elaborate the auxiliary vector, the more likely that the target constraints in (2.7) cannot be satisfied (e.g., due to empty cells).

16 Trimming weights will generally cause the weighted sample to deviate from the population targets.

More generally, it is unwise to select the auxiliary vector based on statistical criteria alone. First, analysts often have theoretical and substantive knowledge of the nonresponse mechanism and of correlates of the outcome of interest, and this prior information should inform the choice of auxiliary vector (Bethlehem, Cobben, and Schouten 2011, 247–287).[17] For example, it may be known that nonresponse tends to be particularly severe among low-education males, in which case the auxiliary vector should include the interaction of gender and education. Second, considerations of interpretability may favor the selection of a simpler auxiliary vector over one that is more powerful but also more complex. This is particularly true of weights that will subsequently be used by other analysts or that must be explained to project sponsors or other non-experts. In such cases, it may be easier to explain weights that match, say, the marginal population distributions of age, gender, education, and state than ones that satisfy a more complicated set of interactions among these variables (e.g., age-by-education in some states but not others).

In sum, the specification of the auxiliary vector should generally be based on a combination of substantive and statistical criteria (subject to practical constraints). One heuristic procedure is the following:

1. Identify the most complex (i.e., most highly interacted) auxiliary vector for which corresponding population targets can be derived from auxiliary information.
2. If calibrating with the most complex vector is infeasible, select a minimal subset of population benchmarks that, for substantive or pragmatic reasons, the weighted sample must match if possible. Marginal benchmarks will often suffice, but it may also be desirable to include certain key interactions known a priori to be important.
3. Identify which feasible additions to the auxiliary vector (if any) substantially increase its ability to predict nonresponse and outcomes of interest, over and above the minimal vector selected in step 2. This may be done through a formal procedure, such as those suggested by Särndal and Lundstrom (2008) and Caughey and Hartman (2017), or through less structured analyses (e.g., a series of regressions involving different candidate auxiliary vectors).
4. Attempt to calibrate the sample using the auxiliary vector selected in steps 1–3. If calibration fails or the resulting weights are unacceptably variable, reformulate the vector (e.g., by removing terms) and try again until calibration succeeds.

As step 4 suggests, selecting an auxiliary vector is often an iterative process of trial and error. That said, it is generally desirable to keep weight estimation

[17] In Caughey and Hartman's approach, the lasso can be forced to select certain variables by setting the penalty for their coefficients to 0 (Caughey and Hartman 2017, 20).

separate from parameter estimation. Otherwise, the researcher may be tempted to cherry-pick the auxiliary vector that yields the "best" (i.e., most publishable) substantive results. In some cases, weights can be validated by comparing weighted and unweighted survey estimates with a population benchmark not included in the population targets. Such out-of-sample validation is fairly rare because the same qualities that make a variable a good benchmark also recommend it for inclusion in the auxiliary vector, but if possible validation can provide compelling support for one's weighting strategy (for examples, see Section 5.3). Finally, it should be noted that the choice of auxiliary vector depends on the intended purpose of the weights – for example, are they general-purpose weights, or will they be used to analyze only a single outcome? To the extent that the latter is true, then the auxiliary vector's ability to predict the outcome of interest becomes correspondingly more important as a selection criterion.

## 2.5 Summary of Weight Estimation

We have shown that the two most common weighting methods, poststratification and raking, can be considered special cases of calibration, a more general weighting framework. Calibration entails weighting the sample so that it matches a specified set of population targets, while deviating as little as possible from the design weights. The population targets may consist of marginal distributions (raking) or cell proportions (poststratification), or indeed any function of one or more auxiliary variables. The extent to which calibration reduces nonresponse bias depends on the extent to which the auxiliary vector (the functions of the auxiliary variables included in the population targets) predicts both nonresponse and the outcome of interest. Automating the specification of auxiliary vectors is a topic of active research, but in most applications this choice should be based on a combination of statistical criteria and substantive knowledge.

## 2.6 Example Code

The Code Ocean capsule for this section is published at `https://doi.org/10.24433/CO.3986927.v1`.

Listing 2.1 Setup

```
## Libraries
library(survey)     # for analyzing complex surveys (see Lumley 2010)

## Read data
gss_df <- readRDS("data/GSS2016_use.rds") # survey data
acs_df <- readRDS("data/ACS2016_use.rds") # auxiliary information

```

```
 8 ## Create design-weighted svydesign objects
 9 gss_dwt <- svydesign(ids = ~vpsu, weights = ~design_wt, strata = ~vstrat,
10                      data = gss_df, nest = TRUE)
11 acs_dwt <- svydesign(ids = ~1, weight = ~perwt, data = acs_df)
12
13 ## Create replicate-weight design (for bootstrapping; see Canty & Davison 1999)
14 gss_boot <- as.svrepdesign(gss_dwt, type = "bootstrap", replicates = 100)
```

Listing 2.2 Function for creating population targets from auxiliary information and formula

```
1 create_targets <- function (target_design, target_formula) {
2     target_mf <- model.frame(target_formula, model.frame(target_design))
3     target_mm <- model.matrix(target_formula, target_mf)
4     wts <- weights(target_design)
5     colSums(target_mm * wts) / sum(wts) # returns vector of targets
6 }
```

Listing 2.3 Poststratification by gender

```
 1 ## Method 1: Calculate weights manually: w_i = (P_i/p_i)*d_i
 2 (male_prop_samp <- svymean(~sex, gss_dwt)["sexmale"]) # sample prop male (wtd)
 3 (male_prop_pop <- svymean(~sex, acs_dwt)["sexmale"])  # target prop male
 4 pswts <- ifelse(gss_dwt$variables$sex == "male",
 5                 (male_prop_pop/male_prop_samp)*weights(gss_dwt),
 6                 ((1 - male_prop_pop)/(1 - male_prop_samp))*weights(gss_dwt))
 7
 8 ### Compare weights of men and women
 9 summary(pswts[gss_dwt$variables$sex == "male"]/mean(pswts))   # underrepresented
10 summary(pswts[gss_dwt$variables$sex == "female"]/mean(pswts)) # overrepresented
11
12 ## Method 2: Poststratification as a form of linear weighting
13 gss_ps <- calibrate(design = gss_dwt,
14                     formula = ~sex,
15                     population = create_targets(acs_dwt, ~sex),
16                     calfun = "linear")
17
18 ## The two methods produce the same (normalized) weights.
19 cor(pswts, weights(gss_ps))
20 all.equal(pswts/mean(pswts), weights(gss_ps)/mean(weights(gss_ps)),
21           check.names = FALSE)
```

Listing 2.4 Calibration

```
 1 ## Formula notation for auxiliary vector (function of auxiliary variables)
 2 target_formula <- ~ (sex + age_int)^2 + I(age_int^2) + race3 + edu5
 3
 4 ## Vector of targets
 5 (targets <- create_targets(acs_dwt, target_formula))
 6
 7 ## Linear weighting
 8 gss_lwt <- calibrate(design = gss_dwt,
 9                      formula = target_formula,
10                      population = targets,
11                      calfun = "linear")
12
13 ## Entropy weighting (like raking but can use continuous variables)
14 gss_ewt <- calibrate(design = gss_dwt,
15                      formula = target_formula,
16                      population = targets,
17                      calfun = "raking")
18
```

```
## Compare weights from different methods (they are very similar)
cor(weights(gss_lwt), weights(gss_ewt))
plot(weights(gss_lwt), weights(gss_ewt))
abline(0, 1)

## Verify targets

### means
svymean(~edu5 + sex + age_int + race3, gss_dwt) # unadjusted
svymean(~edu5 + sex + age_int + race3, acs_dwt) # target
svymean(~edu5 + sex + age_int + race3, gss_lwt) # linear weighting
svymean(~edu5 + sex + age_int + race3, gss_ewt) # entropy weighting

### interaction of sex and age
svyby(~age_int, ~sex, gss_dwt, svymean) # unadjusted
svyby(~age_int, ~sex, acs_dwt, svymean) # target
svyby(~age_int, ~sex, gss_lwt, svymean) # linear weighting
svyby(~age_int, ~sex, gss_ewt, svymean) # entropy weighting

### quantiles
svyquantile(~age_int, gss_dwt, seq(.1, .9, .1)) # unadjusted
svyquantile(~age_int, acs_dwt, seq(.1, .9, .1)) # target
svyquantile(~age_int, gss_lwt, seq(.1, .9, .1)) # linear weighting
svyquantile(~age_int, gss_ewt, seq(.1, .9, .1)) # entropy weighting
```

Listing 2.5 Bootstrapping calibrated survey designs

```
gss_lwt_boot <- as.svrepdesign(gss_lwt, type = "bootstrap", replicates = 100)
svyquantile(~age_int, gss_lwt_boot, q = .5) # bootstrap inference for median
```

## 3 Target Estimation

Until this point, we have assumed that the auxiliary information $\breve{I}_{\boldsymbol{x}}$ consists of the auxiliary variables' joint distribution in the population $f_{\mathcal{U}}(\boldsymbol{x})$ and that this distribution is measured without error. If this is true, then any univariate or multivariate moment of $f_{\mathcal{U}}(\boldsymbol{x})$ can be included in the population targets $\tilde{T}_{\boldsymbol{x}}$, and the sample can be weighted to match these targets (assuming no empty cells or other sparsity constraints). As we have discussed, however, population targets are rarely known with certainty. Rather, they must usually be estimated with the aid of a (perhaps implicit) **measurement model** relating the population distribution $f_{\mathcal{U}}(\boldsymbol{x})$ to the auxiliary information $\breve{I}_{\boldsymbol{x}}$. In other words, auxiliary information is itself an estimate of population quantities, with a degree of error that depends on how the information was measured.

This section discusses the problems that arise in the construction of population targets and reviews potential solutions. It focuses especially on the dynamic ecological inference approach proposed by Caughey and Wang (2019). We emphasize, however, that because **target estimation** has been relatively neglected, how best to approach the problem is still an open question and a subject of ongoing research.

## 3.1 Illustration of the Problem

As motivation, consider the challenge faced by Berinsky et al. (2011) in constructing adjustment weights for quota-sampled opinion polls conducted between 1936 and 1945. These authors knew that, due to a combination of intentional and unintentional sampling biases, the quota samples were unrepresentative of the US adult population with respect to race, region, class, gender, and other characteristics. Since these attributes were also correlated with important political attitudes such as party identification, unweighted sample estimates of these attitudes were likely biased. These scholars therefore sought to weight the samples to be more representative of the target population (US adults) with respect to these characteristics.

In this example, however, the construction of population targets presents several complications, which can be illustrated with the auxiliary variables *Black* (black/non-black), *South* (South/non-South), and *Phone* (phone/non-phone). The first complication is that auxiliary information on these variables had to be obtained from multiple data sources. Data on the first two variables were gathered decennially by the US Census, so for census years their joint population distribution could be estimated with a high degree of precision from **Integrated Public Use Microdata Series (IPUMS)** samples of census records (Ruggles et al. 2010). Data on regional phone ownership rates, however, had to be derived from the records gathered by **American Telephone and Telegraph (AT&T)** in various years. No single data source contained information on the joint distribution of *Black*, *South*, and *Phone* until 1960, the first year the US Census included a question about phone ownership.

The second complication is that the distribution of each of these attributes changed substantially across time. This is especially true of phone ownership, which between 1940 and 1960 increased from 37% to 78% of households (Field 2006), but this period also brought substantial change in regions' relative population sizes as well as in the racial breakdown within regions. Consequently, calibrating to a static set of targets is unlikely to make samples representative of the population at any particular point in time. Further complications are raised by discrepancies between how the sources of auxiliary data measure phone ownership and how opinion polls in this period did so (e.g., at the household versus person level).

Table 3.1, using data from 1940, illustrates the structure of the auxiliary information available in this application. The table presents a $2 \times 2 \times 2$ array of cells defined by *South*, *Black*, and *Phone*. True population proportions are represented by $P$ and (estimated) target proportions by $\breve{P}$. Subscripts indicate the presence (uppercase) or absence (lowercase) of the three attributes, with

**Table 3.1** Phone ownership by race and region in 1940. Unobserved proportions are represented by $P$ and observed proportions by $\breve{P}$. Subscripts indicate the presence (uppercase) or absence (lowercase) of the three attributes.

| | South ($\breve{P}_{S++} = 0.25$) | | | Non-South ($\breve{P}_{s++} = 0.75$) | | |
|---|---|---|---|---|---|---|
| | Phone | Non-Phone | | Phone | Non-Phone | |
| Black | $P_{SBP}$ | $P_{SBp}$ | $\breve{P}_{SB+} = 0.06$ | $P_{sBP}$ | $P_{sBp}$ | $\breve{P}_{sB+} = 0.03$ |
| Non-Black | $P_{SbP}$ | $P_{Sbp}$ | $\breve{P}_{Sb+} = 0.19$ | $P_{sbP}$ | $P_{sbp}$ | $\breve{P}_{sb+} = 0.72$ |
| | $\breve{P}_{S+P} = 0.05$ | $\breve{P}_{S+p} = 0.21$ | | $\breve{P}_{S+P} = 0.30$ | $\breve{P}_{S+p} = 0.45$ | |

a subscript + indicating summation over the levels of the omitted attribute. Formally, the auxiliary information in this example is

$$\begin{aligned} \breve{I}_{\boldsymbol{x}} &= \{\breve{I}_{\boldsymbol{x}}^{\text{IPUMS}}, \breve{I}_{\boldsymbol{x}}^{\text{AT\&T}}\} \\ &= \{(\breve{P}_{SB+}, \breve{P}_{Sb+}, \breve{P}_{sB+}, \breve{P}_{sb+}), (\breve{P}_{S+P}, \breve{P}_{S+p}, \breve{P}_{s+P}, \breve{P}_{s+p})\}. \end{aligned} \tag{3.1}$$

Berinsky et al. thus had auxiliary information on the joint population distributions of *South* and *Black* (from IPUMS) and of *South* and *Phone* (from AT&T) but not the joint distribution of all three variables.

## 3.2 Approaches to Target Estimation

What kinds of population targets could be constructed from the auxiliary information available in the example just described? One approach, the one actually taken in Berinsky et al. (2011), would be to create raking weights based on marginal distributions alone. In this case, the population targets would be

$$\tilde{T}_{\boldsymbol{x}} = \{\tilde{P}_{S++}, \tilde{P}_{+B+}, \tilde{P}_{++P}\}, \tag{3.2}$$

where, for example, $\tilde{P}_{S++} = \breve{P}_{S++}$ represents the proportion of the population that lives in the South (recall that ˘ indicates auxiliary information and ˜ indicates the population targets used to weight). As Section 2.3 explained, raking on the marginal proportions yields consistent estimators if either the response influence $\omega$ or the survey outcome $y$ is explained by a linear combination of the attributes *South*, *Black*, and *Phone*. If, however, both $\omega$ and $y$ depend on interactions among these attributes – because, say, black Southerners were particularly underrepresented in early polls, as they in fact were – then calibrating to the marginal proportions will not in general eliminate bias. Rather, it is necessary to calibrate the sample to the (unobserved) interior cell proportions in Table 3.1.

An alternative approach, suggested by Leeman and Wasserfallen (2017), is to create "synthetic" joint population targets from the observed marginal proportions. The simplest way to do this is to estimate the interior cells in

Table 3.1 as the product of the marginal proportions (Leeman and Wasserfallen also propose more sophisticated variants of this approach). The targets are then

$$\tilde{T}_{x} = \{\tilde{P}_{\mathrm{SBP}}, \tilde{P}_{\mathrm{SBp}}, \tilde{P}_{\mathrm{SbP}}, \tilde{P}_{\mathrm{Sbp}}, \tilde{P}_{\mathrm{sBP}}, \tilde{P}_{\mathrm{sBp}}, \tilde{P}_{\mathrm{sbP}}, \tilde{P}_{\mathrm{sbp}}\}, \tag{3.3}$$

where, for example, non-black Southerners without a phone would be estimated to comprise $\tilde{P}_{\mathrm{Sbp}} = \frac{\breve{P}_{\mathrm{Sb+}}}{\breve{P}_{\mathrm{S++}}} \times \frac{\breve{P}_{\mathrm{S+p}}}{\breve{P}_{\mathrm{S++}}} \times \breve{P}_{\mathrm{S++}} = \frac{0.19}{0.25} \times \frac{0.21}{0.25} \times 0.25 = 16\%$ of the total population. These targets could then be used to poststratify the poll samples to match the (estimated) joint distribution of the three variables.[18] This method is valid under the assumption that *Black* and *Phone* are independent in the population. Both historical intuition and external data suggest that, contrary to this assumption, phone ownership was much lower among blacks than non-blacks. The 1960 IPMUS, for example, reports a phone-ownership rate of 70% among Southern whites versus 39% among Southern blacks.

Ideally, then, one would want to incorporate external information on the population covariance of *Black* and *Phone*. One way to do so would be through model-based imputation. Ansolabehere and Rivers (2013, 314–315), for example, describe how a **synthetic sampling frame (SSF)** can be used as population targets for adjusting survey samples from online panels.[19] The SSF is created by merging multiple government surveys, which are then augmented by imputing additional variables based on the predicted values of a model fit to data from a separate survey containing these variables. The imputed variables' distribution in the SSF thus reflects their covariance with the variables contained in the imputation model. Applying the SSF method to quota-sampled opinion polls would require an external data source, such as a special government survey, from which the phone ownership's relationship with race and region could be modeled and then imputed onto the population targets used for weighting.

None of the methods described in this section addresses the complication of population change, which requires that population targets be dynamic rather than static. When population data are observed in the same form at different points in time, constructing dynamic population targets can be relatively

[18] This simple version of the "synthetic poststratification" method is essentially identical to raking except that it ignores the sample distribution across cells, treating them instead as uniform (i.e., $p_c = n_{\mathcal{R}}^{-1}, \forall c$). This can be seen by substituting into equation (2.5) the solutions $\hat{\lambda}_0 = \log(n_{\mathcal{R}})$, $\hat{\alpha}_r = \log(\breve{P}_{g+})$, and $\hat{\beta}_r = \log(\breve{P}_{+r})$. This yields the maximum likelihood estimates $\tilde{P}^{\mathrm{rake}}_{gr} = n_{\mathcal{R}}^{-1} \exp\{\log(n_{\mathcal{R}}) + \log(\breve{P}_{g+}) + \log(\breve{P}_{+r})\} = \breve{P}_{g+} \times \breve{P}_{+r}\ \forall g, r$, where $\breve{P}_{g+}$ and $\breve{P}_{+r}$ are the marginal population proportions of gender $g$ and race $r$, respectively. These are simply the raking estimates produced by iterative proportional fitting (see Binder and Théberge 1988, 49–50; Little and Wu 1991, 87, equation (5)).

[19] The adjustment is performed through a combination of matching and propensity-score weighting.

straightforward. For example, Enns and Koch (2013) construct dynamic targets for the joint distribution of gender, race, education, and state for the years between 1950 and 2000 by linearly interpolating the cell proportions in decennial IPUMS samples. Similar linear interpolation would be possible for marginal proportions in Table 3.1, though not the interior cells, using census and AT&T data from years before and after 1940. Of course, the accuracy of the interpolated values would depend on whether the rate of change was constant between observed values. While fairly reasonable after 1940, the assumption of linear change is less tenable for earlier years, especially for phone ownership, which actually fell and then recovered during the Depression decade of the 1930s.

## 3.3 Dynamic Ecological Inference

An alternative approach to target estimation, which incorporates elements of several of the approaches reviewed in Section 3.2, couches it as a problem of dynamic **ecological inference (EI)**. In general terms, EI is the drawing of conclusions about individuals from aggregate information (Freedman 2001; King, Rosen, and Tanner 2004). For example, a classic application of EI is estimating the proportion of individuals in different racial categories who register with each political party, given aggregate data on race and party registration. Our goal in this application is analogous: We wish to use aggregate data on the marginal distributions of *Black* and *Phone* within regions to make inferences about the proportion of individuals with each combination of these traits.

Though EI is traditionally applied to data measured at a single point in time, Quinn (2004) has shown that it can be applied to longitudinal data as well. For our purpose, a dynamic approach to EI has two advantages. First, and most obviously, incorporating data from and producing estimates for multiple points in time helps address the problem of population change, which can render static targets inaccurate. Second, data from other time points – even from well outside the period of interest – can be a crucial source of additional information regarding interior cells, without which EI is unreliable (Freedman 2001; Wakefield 2004). This second concern is particularly salient in our application here, for we know from the 1960 IPUMS that race and phone ownership were not independent within regions. By allowing information from later time points to inform estimates for the period of interest (in this case, 1936–1945), a dynamic EI model has the potential to substantially improve the accuracy of population targets.

Caughey and Wang (2019) describe a Bayesian framework for dynamic EI with two basic components. The first component is an **observation model** that links the auxiliary information to the population proportions at a given point in time. The second is a **transition model** that characterizes the evolution of the population proportions across time periods. Through these two models, the estimates at a given time point are jointly informed by the data available at that time point and the estimates for other periods, which are themselves informed by data from other periods. In this way, data from the past or future (e.g., the 1960 IPUMS) indirectly inform estimates for periods when less detailed data are available.

Formally, for each period $t$ and data source $m$, the observation model can be written as

$$\breve{\boldsymbol{n}}_{tm}^{\text{aux}} \sim \text{multinomial}(\boldsymbol{A}_{tm}\boldsymbol{P}_t,\ n_{tm}^{\text{aux}}) \tag{3.4}$$

where $n_{tm}^{\text{aux}}$ is the sample size of the auxiliary data source, $\breve{\boldsymbol{n}}_{tm}^{\text{aux}} = \lceil \breve{\boldsymbol{P}}_{tm} \times n_{tm}^{\text{aux}} \rfloor$ is a vector of (rounded) marginal totals from the auxiliary data, $\boldsymbol{P}_t$ is a vector of cell proportions, and $\boldsymbol{A}_{tm}$ is an indicator matrix whose multiplication with $\boldsymbol{P}_t$ has the effect of summing $\boldsymbol{P}_t$ across the margins represented in $\breve{\boldsymbol{P}}_{tm}$. The sampling process is modeled with the **Multinomial** distribution, whose variance is inversely proportional to the sample size, $n_{tm}^{\text{aux}}$.[20] So, for example, a million-observation microsample from the 1940 US Census containing the variables *South* and *Black* would yield $n_{tm}^{\text{aux}} = 10^6$ and marginal proportions $\breve{P}_{tm} = (\breve{P}_{\text{SB}+},\ \breve{P}_{\text{Sb}+},\ \breve{P}_{\text{sB}+},\ \breve{P}_{\text{sb}+})$ and would have an indicator matrix of the form

$$\boldsymbol{A}_{tm} = \begin{pmatrix} 1 & 1 & 0 & 0 & 0 & 0 & 0 & 0 \\ 0 & 0 & 1 & 1 & 0 & 0 & 0 & 0 \\ 0 & 0 & 0 & 0 & 1 & 1 & 0 & 0 \\ 0 & 0 & 0 & 0 & 0 & 0 & 1 & 1 \end{pmatrix}.$$

Under the Multinomial observation model, the expected value of $\breve{P}_{\text{SB}+}$, for example, is $P_{\text{SBP}}+P_{\text{SBp}}$, from which $\breve{P}_{\text{SB}+}$ differs due only to sampling variability. Thus, absent further information, the model informs estimates of the sum of population cells across the given margins but does not place any constraints on the cell proportions within the marginal categories (e.g., the phone-ownership rate among Southern blacks).

Further information can come from two sources: additional auxiliary data from the same period (e.g., AT&T data on phone ownership) or estimates from other periods. The latter information is transmitted via the transition model:

[20] The observation model in (3.4) can also be written as a Dirichlet distribution. This has the advantage of avoiding rounding, though the Dirichlet cannot be used if $\breve{\boldsymbol{P}}_{tm}$ contains 0s (i.e., if there are any empty cells in the auxiliary data).

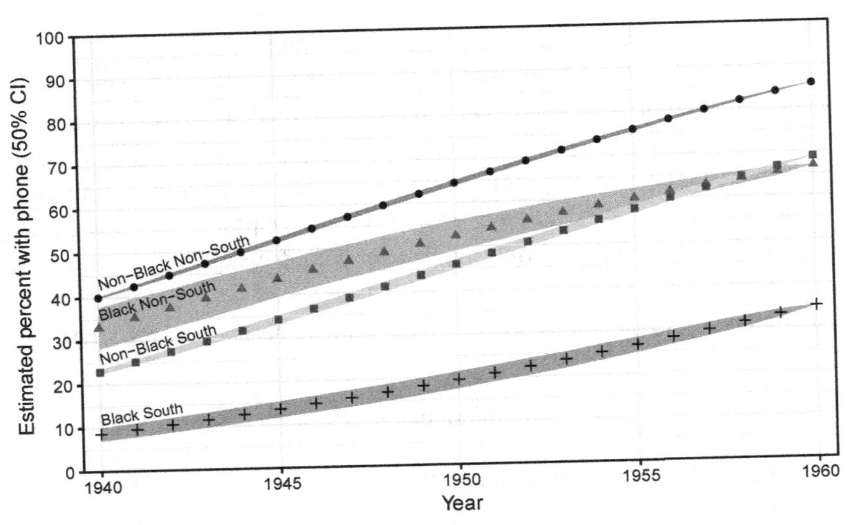


**Figure 3.1** Estimated phone ownership by race and region, 1940–1960.

$$\boldsymbol{P}_t \sim \text{Dir}(\boldsymbol{P}_{t-1} n^{\text{evol}}), \tag{3.5}$$

where Dir denotes the **Dirichlet** distribution, which is closely related to the Multinomial. In the Dirichlet transition model, the expected value of $\boldsymbol{P}_t$ is $\boldsymbol{P}_{t-1}$, and the transition variance is inversely proportional to $n^{\text{evol}}$ (which would typically be set by the user). The transition model thus serves as a prior distribution for $P_t$, propagating information forwards and backwards in time. If data distinguishing two cells are available in one year (e.g., 1960) but not in others (e.g., 1940), the cell estimates in other years will nonetheless differ from one another due to the information conveyed through the transition model.

Figure 3.1 reports the results of a dynamic EI model estimated using the marginal data reported in Table 3.1 plus the full three-way cross-tabulation from the 1960 IPUMS. The figure plots the estimated percentage of phone owners in each race-region category in each year between 1940 and 1960. Even though the data for 1940 contain no information on phone ownership by race within each region, the estimates for 1940 nonetheless show a clear gap between blacks and non-blacks. This is because transition model propagates the information contained in the 1960 IMPUS backwards in time. The result is that estimates for the period of interest (circa 1940) more accurately reflect the joint distribution of *South*, *Black*, and *Phone*. These estimates (or functions thereof) can then be used as dynamic population targets for calibration of poll samples.

## 3.4 Uncertainty in Population Targets

Whether they are estimated from a model or calculated directly from auxiliary data, population targets are usually subject to some uncertainty. It is often possible to estimate the magnitude of this uncertainty from the sample size and sampling design of the auxiliary data source (e.g., if the auxiliary data are from another survey) or from the results of an EI or other measurement model. Uncertainty estimates may also reflect subjective judgment about the targets' reliability (e.g., in the case of auxiliary information derived from expert estimates). In practice, almost all empirical applications ignore uncertainty in population targets. One reason for this may be that nearly every textbook treats targets as known rather than estimated (but see Valliant, Dever, and Kreuter 2018). Recently, however, survey statisticians have begun to consider the problem of uncertain population targets from a variety of angles.

One line of research focuses on how the use of estimated targets can inflate the variance of calibration estimators. Dever and Valliant (2010), for example, show that if targets are estimated and the auxiliary data source is not substantially larger than the survey sample, variance estimates for the conventional poststratification estimator can exhibit severe negative bias. They propose jackknife-based variance estimators that mitigate this downward bias. In subsequent work, Dever and Valliant (2016) extend these results to the **generalized regression (GREG)** estimator,

$$\begin{aligned} \hat{\mu}_y^{\text{GREG}} &= \hat{\mu}_y^{\text{H}} + (\tilde{\boldsymbol{\mu}}_{\mathbf{z}} - \hat{\boldsymbol{\mu}}_{\mathbf{z}}^{\text{H}})' \hat{\boldsymbol{B}}_{\mathcal{R}} \\ &= \hat{\mu}_y^{\text{H}} + (\tilde{\boldsymbol{\mu}}_{\mathbf{z}} - \hat{\boldsymbol{\mu}}_{\mathbf{z}}^{\text{H}})' \left[ \sum_{i \in \mathcal{R}} d_i \mathbf{z}_i \mathbf{z}_i' \right]^{-1} \left[ \sum_{i \in \mathcal{R}} d_i \mathbf{z}_i y_i \right] \end{aligned} \tag{3.6}$$

a form of **linear weighting** that includes poststratification as a special case.[21] Särndal and Traat (2011) consider calibration estimation of subpopulations from a similar perspective.

The aforementioned works employ estimators that simply substitute the estimated targets where known ones would ordinarily be. Greater efficiency can be obtained, however, by altering the estimator to account for uncertainty in

[21] Deville and Särndal (1992, 376–377). GREG implies the calibration weights

$$w_i = d_i(1 + \mathbf{z}_i' \boldsymbol{\lambda}) \quad \forall i \in \mathcal{R},$$

where

$$\boldsymbol{\lambda} = \left( \sum_{i \in \mathcal{R}} d_i \mathbf{z}_i \mathbf{z}_i' \right)^{-1} N \left( \tilde{\boldsymbol{\mu}}_{\mathbf{z}} - \hat{\boldsymbol{\mu}}_{\mathbf{z}}^{\text{H}} \right).$$

the targets. In the case of GREG, doing so results in a ridge regression version of (3.6) in which the coefficients $\hat{\boldsymbol{B}}_{\mathcal{R}}$ are penalized in proportion to the targets' uncertainty (Deville 2000, 208). The "ridge" GREG estimator, which under certain assumptions is maximally efficient, implicitly calibrates the sample to an alternative set of targets,

$$\tilde{\boldsymbol{\mu}}_{\boldsymbol{z}}^{*} = \hat{\boldsymbol{\Lambda}}\tilde{\boldsymbol{\mu}}_{\boldsymbol{z}} + (\boldsymbol{I} - \hat{\boldsymbol{\Lambda}})\hat{\boldsymbol{\mu}}_{\boldsymbol{z}}^{\mathrm{H}}, \tag{3.7}$$

where $\boldsymbol{I}$ is an identity matrix and $\hat{\boldsymbol{\Lambda}} = \widehat{\mathrm{var}}(\hat{\boldsymbol{\mu}}_{\boldsymbol{z}}^{\mathrm{H}}) \;/\; \left[\widehat{\mathrm{var}}(\tilde{\boldsymbol{\mu}}_{\boldsymbol{z}}) + \widehat{\mathrm{var}}(\hat{\boldsymbol{\mu}}_{\boldsymbol{z}}^{\mathrm{H}})\right]$ indexes the uncertainty of the sample estimates of $\boldsymbol{\mu}_{\boldsymbol{z}}$ relative to the uncertainty of the corresponding targets (Guandalini and Tillé 2017, 257). The modified targets $\tilde{\boldsymbol{\mu}}_{\boldsymbol{z}}^{*}$ are thus precision-weighted averages of the target and sample estimates. As $\widehat{\mathrm{var}}(\tilde{\boldsymbol{\mu}}_{\boldsymbol{z}})$ tends to 0 (its value when the targets are known with certainty), $\hat{\boldsymbol{\Lambda}}$ converges on the identity matrix and the modified estimator reduces to classic GREG calibrated on $\tilde{\boldsymbol{\mu}}_{\boldsymbol{z}}$.

In practice, it is not always obvious whether it is better to calibrate to the observed targets $\tilde{\boldsymbol{\mu}}_{\boldsymbol{z}}$ or to the precision-weighted targets $\tilde{\boldsymbol{\mu}}_{\boldsymbol{z}}^{*}$ defined in (3.7). Both estimators are asymptotically unbiased under conditions similar to those described in Section 2.3 (Dever and Valliant 2016, 296–297). The efficiency properties used to justify ridge GREG are derived under the assumption of probability sampling with full response.[22] In the presence of nonresponse, it may be better from a bias perspective to calibrate to $\tilde{\boldsymbol{\mu}}_{\boldsymbol{z}}$ rather let the targets be informed by the (biased) sample estimates $\hat{\boldsymbol{\mu}}_{\boldsymbol{z}}^{\mathrm{H}}$. In any case, simulations reported by Dever and Valliant (2016, 305) suggest that calibrating to any reasonably reliable set of targets substantially reduces the bias of survey estimators relative to no calibration at all.

An additional practical consideration is that analytical formulas for point and variance estimators in the presence of uncertain targets are not available for all forms of calibration (e.g., raking). However, a general algorithm for propagating uncertainty in the targets, **method of composition (MOC)**, can be applied to essentially any calibration (or other) estimator (Tanner 1996, 52–54; Treier and Jackman 2008, 215–216; for code, see Listing 3.7). MOC estimates the marginal distribution of a parameter by using Monte Carlo simulation to integrate over uncertainty in the data used to estimate the parameter. Denote the estimated measurement-error distribution of the targets $\tilde{T}_{\boldsymbol{x}}$ as $\tilde{p}(\tilde{T}_{\boldsymbol{x}})$, and let $\hat{p}(\hat{\theta}_y \mid \tilde{T}_{\boldsymbol{x}})$ denote the estimated sampling distribution of the survey estimate $\hat{\theta}_y$ conditional on the population targets. The marginal distribution $\hat{p}(\hat{\theta}_y) = \int \hat{p}(\hat{\theta}_y \mid \tilde{T}_{\boldsymbol{x}})\tilde{p}(\tilde{T}_{\boldsymbol{x}})d\tilde{T}_{\boldsymbol{x}}$ can be estimated via the following two-step algorithm. For each iteration $s \in \{1 \ldots S\}$:

[22] This is true at least of Guandalini and Tillé (2017, 251). The point is less clear in Deville (2000).

1. Draw one value $\tilde{T}_{\boldsymbol{x}}^{(s)}$ from $\tilde{p}(\tilde{T}_{\boldsymbol{x}})$.
2. Given the sampled value $\tilde{T}_{\boldsymbol{x}}^{(s)}$:
   (a) Estimate $\hat{p}^{(s)}\left(\hat{\theta}_y \mid \tilde{T}_{\boldsymbol{x}}^{(s)}\right)$.
   (b) Draw one value $\hat{\theta}_y^{(s)}$ from $\hat{p}^{(s)}\left(\hat{\theta}_y \mid \tilde{T}_{\boldsymbol{x}}^{(s)}\right)$.

Each value $\hat{\theta}_y^{(s)}$ will be a draw from the marginal distribution $\hat{p}(\hat{\theta}_y)$, and as $S$ grows the set of sampled values will approximate $\hat{p}(\hat{\theta}_y)$ increasingly closely.

If $p(\hat{\theta}_y|\tilde{T}_{\boldsymbol{x}})$ cannot be estimated analytically, the bootstrap could be employed instead. In this case, $\hat{\theta}_y^{(s)}$ in step 2 would be replaced with its value in one bootstrap sample from the survey data (still calculated using $\tilde{T}_{\boldsymbol{x}}^{(s)}$). Repeating this $S$ times would also yield $S$ samples from $\hat{p}(\hat{\theta}_y)$. This modified MOC procedure essentially combines a parametric bootstrap (Davison and Hinkley 1997, 11–21) in step 1 with a nonparametric bootstrap in step 2.

For a practical illustration of MOC, consider the task of poststratifying a survey sample $\mathcal{R}$ to match the partisan distribution in the US population, as estimated by another (more accurate) survey (see. Kastellec et al. 2015). From this benchmark survey, we obtain $\tilde{T}_{\boldsymbol{x}} = \tilde{\mathbf{P}} \equiv (\tilde{P}_{\text{D}}, \tilde{P}_{\text{I}}, \tilde{P}_{\text{R}})$, the vector of estimated proportions of Democrats, Independents, and Republicans in the population. In large samples, $\tilde{p}(\tilde{T}_{\boldsymbol{x}}) = \tilde{p}(\tilde{\mathbf{P}})$ should be well approximated by the multivariate normal distribution $\text{N}_3(\tilde{\mathbf{P}},\ \tilde{\Sigma}_{\tilde{\mathbf{P}}})$, where $\tilde{\Sigma}_{\tilde{\mathbf{P}}}$ is the estimated covariance of $\tilde{\mathbf{P}}$. We therefore draw $S$ =10,000 samples from $\text{N}_3(\tilde{\mathbf{P}},\ \tilde{\Sigma}_{\tilde{\mathbf{P}}})$. With each draw $\tilde{\mathbf{P}}^{(s)}$, we calculate poststratification weights $\tilde{w}_i^{(s)} = (\tilde{P}_{c[i]}^{(s)}/\hat{P}_{c[i]}^{\text{H}})d_i\ \forall i \in \mathcal{R}$ and a poststratification estimate $\hat{\theta}_y^{(s)} = \sum_{\mathcal{R}} \tilde{w}_i^{(s)} y_i / \sum_{\mathcal{R}} \tilde{w}_i^{(s)}$, which too has an approximately normal distribution, $\text{N}(\hat{\theta}_y^{(s)}, \hat{\sigma}^2_{\hat{\theta}_y})$. Then, for each $s$ we draw one value $\hat{\theta}_y^{*(s)}$ from $\text{N}(\hat{\theta}_y^{(s)}, \hat{\sigma}^2_{\hat{\theta}_y}) = \hat{p}^{(s)}\left(\hat{\theta}_y \mid \tilde{\mathbf{P}}^{(s)}\right) = \hat{p}^{(s)}\left(\hat{\theta}_y \mid \tilde{T}_{\boldsymbol{x}}^{(s)}\right)$. The resulting vector $\hat{\boldsymbol{\theta}}_y^*$ comprises 10,000 independent draws from the marginal distribution $\hat{p}(\hat{\theta}_y)$.

## 3.5 Summary of Target Estimation

Target estimation, being much less studied than weight estimation, is a more open and unsettled topic. Guidelines and best practices are generally unavailable. Nevertheless, several lessons do present themselves. The most basic is that auxiliary information cannot usually be taken as a complete and faithful portrait of the target population. Rather, auxiliary information is typically fragmentary and subject to various sources of both systematic and random measurement error. Its temporal coverage also frequently fails to match that of the survey data being analyzed. Addressing these issues requires, at the very least, explicit justification of measurement assumptions and perhaps a full-fledged model linking the auxiliary information to the population of interest. Uncertainty in the population targets, if substantial, should be addressed as well. This section has discussed several potential solutions, but using a specific method is less important than acknowledging these issues and taking reasonable step to ameliorate them.

## 3.6 Example Code

The Code Ocean capsule for this section is published at `https://doi.org/10.24433/CO.7194431.v1`.

Listing 3.1 Setup

```
1  set.seed(1)                                # for reproducibility
2
3  ## Libraries
4  library(tidyverse)                         # for useful utilities
5  library(haven)                             # for reading Stata files
6  library(survey)                            # for analyzing complex surveys
7  library(rstan)                             # for Bayesian simulation
8  library(parallel)                          # for parallel processing (optional)
9  ### If the package `estsubpop` is not installed, run the following line:
10 devtools::install_github("devincaughey/estsubpop")
11 library(estsubpop)                         # for dynamic ecological inference
12
13 ## Options
14 rstan_options(auto_write = TRUE)           # to avoid recompilation
15 options(mc.cores = detectCores())          # to run on multiple cores (optional)
16
17 ## Function for creating targets
18 create_targets <- function (target_design, target_formula) {
19     target_mf <- model.frame(target_formula, model.frame(target_design))
20     target_mm <- model.matrix(target_formula, target_mf)
21     wts <- weights(target_design)
22     colSums(target_mm * wts) / sum(wts) # returns vector of targets
23 }
24
25 ## Auxiliary information
26 st_race_tab <- readRDS("data/st_race_tab.rds")                # 1930-2016
27 st_race_phone_tab <- readRDS("data/st_race_phone_tab.rds")    # 1960-1990
28 phone40_tab <- readRDS("data/phone40_tab.rds")                # 1940
29 phone40_tab$PHONE <- factor(phone40_tab$PHONE)
30
31 ## Survey data (AIPO #380, October 1946)
32 aipo0380 <- read_dta("data/AIPO0380FW.dta") %>%
33     filter(!is.na(SOUTH) & !is.na(BLACK) & !is.na(PHONE)) %>%
34     mutate_if(is.labelled, as_factor)
35
36 aipo0380$SOUTH <- factor(aipo0380$SOUTH, labels = levels(st_race_tab$SOUTH))
37 aipo0380$BLACK <- factor(aipo0380$BLACK, labels = levels(st_race_tab$BLACK))
38 aipo0380$PHONE <- factor(aipo0380$PHONE, labels = levels(phone40_tab$PHONE))
39
40 ## Survey designs
41 phone40_ds <- svydesign(ids = ~1, weights = ~Freq, data = phone40_tab)
42 st_race_ds <- svydesign(ids = ~1, weights = ~Freq, data = st_race_tab)
43 st_race_phone_ds <- svydesign(ids = ~1, weights = ~Freq,
44                               data = st_race_phone_tab)
45 aipo0380_srs <- svydesign(~1, data = aipo0380) # assumes simple random sampling
```

Listing 3.2 Option 1: Use one-way margins as targets

```
### Create targets
(margins_south_1940 <- create_targets(subset(st_race_ds, YEAR == 1940), ~SOUTH))
(margins_black_1940 <- create_targets(subset(st_race_ds, YEAR == 1940), ~BLACK))
(margins_phone_1940 <- create_targets(phone40_ds, ~PHONE))
margins_1940 <- c(margins_south_1940, margins_black_1940, margins_phone_1940)
margins_1940 <- margins_1940[!duplicated(names(margins_1940))]

### Weight (i.e., rake) using marginal targets
aipo0380_mar <- calibrate(design = aipo0380_srs,
                          formula = ~SOUTH + BLACK + PHONE,
                          population = margins_1940,
                          calfun = "raking")
```

Listing 3.3 Option 2: Use “synthetic” cell proportions as targets (equivalent to raking with uniform base weights)

```
### Create synthetic targets
#### Tables containing marginal proportions
xt_s40 <- svytable(~SOUTH, subset(st_race_ds, YEAR == 1940), Ntotal = 1) %>%
    as.data.frame()
xt_b40 <- svytable(~BLACK, subset(st_race_ds, YEAR == 1940), Ntotal = 1) %>%
    as.data.frame()
xt_p40 <- svytable(~PHONE, subset(phone40_ds, YEAR == 1940), Ntotal = 1) %>%
    as.data.frame()
#### Assign each cell a proportion estimated from the marginals
combos <- expand.grid(lapply(aipo0380[c("SOUTH", "BLACK", "PHONE")], levels))
combos$Freq <- NA
for (i in 1:nrow(combos)) {
    p_s <- xt_s40$Freq[xt_s40$SOUTH == combos$SOUTH[i]]
    p_b <- xt_b40$Freq[xt_b40$BLACK == combos$BLACK[i]]
    p_p <- xt_p40$Freq[xt_p40$PHONE == combos$PHONE[i]]
    combos$Freq[i] <- p_s * p_b * p_p
}
#### Convert to targets
combos_ds <- svydesign(~1, weights = ~Freq, data = combos)
synth_targets <- create_targets(combos_ds, ~SOUTH * BLACK * PHONE)

### Weight (i.e., postratify) using synthetic targets
aipo0380_syn1 <- calibrate(design = aipo0380_srs,
                           formula = ~SOUTH * BLACK * PHONE,
                           population = synth_targets,
                           calfun = "raking") # "linear" gives exact same result

### Poststratifying to synthetic targets is equivalent to raking a sample with
### equal-sized cells (i.e., ignoring cell sizes in the sample)
aipo0380_unif <- postStratify(design = aipo0380_srs,
                              strata = ~SOUTH * BLACK * PHONE,
                              population = mutate(combos, Freq = 1))
svytable(~SOUTH + BLACK + PHONE, aipo0380_unif) # weighted cell sizes all equal

aipo0380_syn2 <- calibrate(design = aipo0380_unif,
                           formula = ~SOUTH + BLACK + PHONE,
                           population = margins_1940,
                           calfun = "raking")

all.equal(weights(aipo0380_syn1), weights(aipo0380_syn2), tolerance = .00001,
          check.attributes = FALSE)     # same
all.equal(weights(aipo0380_mar), weights(aipo0380_syn2), tolerance = .00001,
          check.attributes = FALSE)     # different
```

Listing 3.4 Option 3: Weight to two-way margins

```
1  ### Create targets
2  margins_south_black_1940 <-
3      create_targets(subset(st_race_ds, YEAR == 1940), ~SOUTH * BLACK)
4  margins_south_phone_1940 <- create_targets(phone40_ds, ~SOUTH * PHONE)
5  margins_1940_2wy <- c(margins_south_black_1940, margins_south_phone_1940)
6  margins_1940_2wy <- margins_1940_2wy[!duplicated(names(margins_1940_2wy))]
7
8  ### Weight (i.e., rake) to two-way marginals
9  aipo0380_2wy <- calibrate(design = aipo0380_srs,
10                           formula = ~(SOUTH + BLACK)^2 + (SOUTH + PHONE)^2,
11                           population = margins_1940_2wy,
12                           calfun = "raking")
13
14 summary(weights(aipo0380_2wy) / mean(weights(aipo0380_2wy))) # extreme weights
```

Listing 3.5 Option 4: Dynamic ecological inference

```
1  ## Design objects
2  d_ls <- list(phone40_ds,
3               subset(st_race_ds, YEAR %in% 1940),        # use only 1940 info
4               subset(st_race_phone_ds, YEAR %in% 1960)) # use only 1960 info
5
6  ## Formulas for auxiliary vectors (order must correspond to designs).
7  ### Note that here we follow the syntax for `svytable`, in which `+` indicates
8  ### interaction. Separate marginals are indicated with separate formulas, as in
9  ### `list(~PHONE, ~SOUTH)`, though this should rarely be needed.
10 f_ls <- list(list(~PHONE + SOUTH),          # `phone40_ds`
11              list(~BLACK + SOUTH),          # `st_race_ds`
12              list(~PHONE + BLACK + SOUTH)) # `st_race_phone_ds`
13
14 ## Arguments for est_subpop
15 args_ls <- list(
16     periods_to_est = 1940:1960,          # years we want estimates for
17     design_ls = d_ls,                    # list of survey designs
18     formulae_ls = f_ls,                  # list of formulas
19     pi_prior = "uniform",                # prior for cell probabilities
20     n_prior = "vague",                   # precision of cell priors
21     n_evolve_meanlog = 10,               # sets n^evolve to e^10...
22     n_evolve_sdlog = NULL,               # ...with no prior uncertainty
23     verbosity = 1,                       # give me info
24     sampling_model = "multinomial",      # alternative: "dirichlet"
25                                          # args below passed to rstan::sampling
26     control = list(adapt_delta = .9, max_treedepth = 10),
27     chains = 4,
28     iter = 10000,
29     refresh = 100,
30     thin = 1,
31     seed = 1980)
32
33 ## Estimate model
34 est_out <- do.call(est_subpop, args_ls) # takes about 2 minutes per chain
35
36 ## Check sampling diagnostics
37 print(est_out$stan_out)
38
39 ## Extract estimated proportions
40 pi_samps <- estsubpop::get_pi(est_out)
41
42 ## Summarize proportions
43 pi_summ <- pi_samps %>%
44     group_by(PHONE, BLACK, SOUTH, Period) %>%
45     summarise(post_mean = mean(value),  # point estimate
```

```
46                 post_sd = sd(value),       # Bayesian standard error
47                 post_q05 = quantile(value, .05), # Bayesian confidence interval
48                 post_q95 = quantile(value, .95))
49
50 ## Calculate phone ownership percentages
51 phone_samps <- pi_samps %>%
52     filter(iterations %in% seq(1, max(iterations), 100)) %>% # subset for speed
53     group_by(BLACK, SOUTH, Period, chains, iterations) %>% # within iteration
54     summarise(phone_pct = 100 * value[PHONE == "Phone"] / # ... calc group pct
55               (value[PHONE == "Phone"] + value[PHONE == "No Phone"]))
56
57 ## Summarize phone ownership percentages (for 1940 and 1960)
58 phone_samps %>%
59     group_by(SOUTH, BLACK, Period) %>%
60     summarise(phone_pct_q05 = quantile(phone_pct, .05),
61               phone_pct_q50 = quantile(phone_pct, .50),
62               phone_pct_q95 = quantile(phone_pct, .95)) %>%
63     filter(Period %in% c(1940, 1960))
64
65 ## Weight to match estimated targets
66
67 dei_ds <- svydesign(~1, weights = ~post_mean, data = pi_summ)
68
69 ### Calibrate to targets for 1940 (for comparison with weights created above)
70 dei_targets_1940 <-
71     create_targets(subset(dei_ds, Period == 1940), ~SOUTH * BLACK * PHONE)
72 aipo0380_dei40 <- calibrate(design = aipo0380_srs,
73                             formula = ~SOUTH * BLACK * PHONE,
74                             population = dei_targets_1940,
75                             calfun = "raking")
76
77 ### Calibrate to targets for 1946 (when poll was actually conducted)
78 dei_targets_1946 <-
79     create_targets(subset(dei_ds, Period == 1946), ~SOUTH * BLACK * PHONE)
80 aipo0380_dei46 <- calibrate(design = aipo0380_srs,
81                             formula = ~SOUTH * BLACK * PHONE,
82                             population = dei_targets_1946,
83                             calfun = "raking")
```

Listing 3.6 Compare results of weighting to different targets

```
1  ## Marginal distributions
2  margins_1940                                      # marginal targets (1940)
3  svymean(~SOUTH + BLACK + PHONE, aipo0380_srs)     # unweighted
4  svymean(~SOUTH + BLACK + PHONE, aipo0380_mar)     # one-way marginals (1940)
5  svymean(~SOUTH + BLACK + PHONE, aipo0380_syn1)    # synthetic (1940)
6  svymean(~SOUTH + BLACK + PHONE, aipo0380_2wy)     # two-way marginals (1940)
7  svymean(~SOUTH + BLACK + PHONE, aipo0380_dei40)   # dynamic EI (1940)
8  svymean(~SOUTH + BLACK + PHONE, aipo0380_dei46)   # dynamic EI (1946)
9
10 ## Distribution of PHONE by SOUTH and BLACK
11 svyby(~PHONE, by = ~BLACK + SOUTH, aipo0380_srs, svymean)    # unweighted
12 svyby(~PHONE, by = ~BLACK + SOUTH, aipo0380_mar, svymean)    # one-way (1940)
13 svyby(~PHONE, by = ~BLACK + SOUTH, aipo0380_syn1, svymean)   # synthetic (1940)
14 svyby(~PHONE, by = ~BLACK + SOUTH, aipo0380_2wy, svymean)    # two-way (1940)
15 svyby(~PHONE, by = ~BLACK + SOUTH, aipo0380_dei40, svymean)  # dynamic EI (1940)
16 svyby(~PHONE, by = ~BLACK + SOUTH, aipo0380_dei46, svymean)  # dynamic EI (1946)
17
18 ## Party identification
19 calc_dem_rep_diff <- function (design) {
20     svycontrast(svymean(~PID3, design, na.rm = TRUE),
21                 quote(PID3Democrat - PID3Republican))
22 }
23 calc_dem_rep_diff(aipo0380_srs)             # est = -1% (SE = 1.7%)
```

```
24 calc_dem_rep_diff(aipo0380_mar)          # est = +10% (SE = 2.0%)
25 calc_dem_rep_diff(aipo0380_syn1)
26 calc_dem_rep_diff(aipo0380_2wy)
27 calc_dem_rep_diff(aipo0380_dei40)
28 calc_dem_rep_diff(aipo0380_dei46)        # est = +5% (SE = 2.7%)
29 ### Whether and how to weight makes a big difference in this case!
```

Listing 3.7 Propagating uncertainty in the population targets

```
1  ### Sample 1000 iterations from population targets
2  pi_samps <- mutate(pi_samps, chain_iter = interaction(chains, iterations))
3  chain_iter_sample <- sample(levels(pi_samps$chain_iter), 1000)
4  pi_samps_subset <- filter(pi_samps, chain_iter %in% chain_iter_sample)
5
6  ### Use method of composition to propagate uncertainty
7  est_samps <- vector(mode = "list", length = length(chain_iter_sample))
8  boot_samps <- vector(mode = "list", length = length(chain_iter_sample))
9  for (s in seq_along(chain_iter_sample)) { # For each iteration s:
10     if (!s %% 50) print(s)
11     ## (1) Draw one value from p(T);
12     pi_samps_s <- filter(pi_samps, chain_iter == chain_iter_sample[s])
13     pop_s <- svydesign(~1, weights = ~value, data = pi_samps_s)
14     T_s <- create_targets(subset(pop_s, Period == 1946), ~SOUTH * BLACK * PHONE)
15     ## (2a) Option A: Sample from parametric approximation to p(theta | T_s).
16     ##   (i) Estimate theta_s and Cov(theta_s) conditional on T_s
17     ds_s <- calibrate(design = aipo0380_srs,
18                       formula = ~SOUTH * BLACK * PHONE,
19                       population = T_s,
20                       calfun = "raking")
21     stat_s <- svymean(~PID3, ds_s, na.rm = TRUE)
22     ##   (ii) Sample \tilde{theta_s} from MV(\hat{theta_s}, \hat{Cov(theta_s)})
23     est_s <- MASS::mvrnorm(n = 1, mu = as.numeric(stat_s), Sigma = vcov(stat_s))
24     est_samps[[s]] <- est_s
25     ## (2b) Option B: Use bootstrap.
26     boot_s <- svymean(~PID3,
27                       as.svrepdesign(ds_s, type = "bootstrap", replicates = 1),
28                       na.rm = TRUE, return.replicates = TRUE)
29     boot_samps[[s]] <- as.numeric(boot_s$replicates)
30     names(boot_samps[[s]]) <- names(boot_s$mean)
31 }
32
33 ## parametric MOC
34 names(est_samps) <- chain_iter_sample
35 est_df <- as.data.frame(est_samps)
36 ## bootstrap MOC
37 names(boot_samps) <- chain_iter_sample
38 moc_boot_df <- as.data.frame(boot_samps)
39
40 aipo0380_dei46_boot <-
41     as.svrepdesign(aipo0380_dei46, "bootstrap", replicates = 1000)
42
43 tibble(PID = levels(aipo0380$PID3),
44        orig_se = sqrt(diag(vcov(svymean(~PID3, aipo0380_dei46, na.rm = TRUE)))),
45        moc_par_se = apply(est_df, 1, sd),
46        orig_boot_se = sqrt(diag(vcov(svymean(~PID3, aipo0380_dei46_boot,
47                                              na.rm = TRUE)))),
48        moc_boot_se = apply(moc_boot_df, 1, sd))
49 ### In this case, because the uncertainty in the targets is so small,
50 ### propagating the uncertainty barely affects the estimated standard errors.
```

## 4 Application to Contemporary Election Surveys

This section and the one that follows illustrate the workflow we have described in two empirical applications: a telephone-based pre-election survey from 2016 that employed **random digit dialing (RDD)** and face-to-face opinion polls from the 1930s–1950s in which respondents were selected using **quota sampling**. Despite the gap in time separating these surveys and the methodological differences between them, they present a surprisingly similar set of problems for the survey analyst. These applications are designed to highlight the general tasks and decisions entailed by target and weight estimation and also to illustrate (using R code) how in practice to implement the methods we have described in the preceding sections.

* * *

Elections in 2016 were not kind to pollsters, who suffered several embarrassing failures. In the United Kingdom, opinion polls taken just before a 2016 referendum on the European Union systematically underestimated support for leaving the union, with most point predictions suggesting erroneously that "Remain" would prevail (British Polling Council 2016). Just a few months later, Donald Trump defied most poll-based forecasts by defeating Hillary Clinton in the US presidential election (Kennedy et al. 2018). These high-profile mistakes, though understandable given the closeness of the contests involved, highlight the continuing challenges of polling in the twenty-first century.

This section explores adjustment weighting's potential for improving political polling. Of course, in this era of low response rates, nearly all survey organizations use some sort of weighting. The question, therefore, is not *whether* to weight but *how* to do so. As we demonstrate, the choice of exactly how to weight can greatly affect the accuracy of the results. Indeed, weighting is by no means guaranteed to yield better estimates. We illustrate this with a retrospective analysis of a survey fielded shortly before the 2016 US presidential election. This exercise is unfair in the sense that it takes advantage of information about nonresponse and other problems that were not fully understood before the election. It should thus be taken not so much as criticism of pollsters' performance in 2016 as an illustration of how the combination of auxiliary information and substantive knowledge can improve public opinion polling.

### 4.1 Retrospective Adjustment of a Pre-Election Survey

In a comprehensive review of polling in the 2016 election, Kennedy et al. (2018) attribute polls' systematic underestimation of Trump's support to three major factors: (1) failure to adjust for the overrepresentation of college-educated whites; (2) a late break towards Trump among undecided voters; and, less certainly, (3) misspecification of likely-voter models. Although the second and third factors are undeniably consequential for prospective analysis, we assume them away in this analysis by defining the target population as the actual 2016 electorate, which of course was not known before the election. We focus instead on the first factor, which resulted from the fact that most pollsters did not weight their samples by education, a strong predictor of both vote choice and nonresponse. With the benefit of hindsight, can this knowledge improve the (retrospective) predictive accuracy of pre-election surveys?

### 4.1.1 Survey Data

To investigate this question, we analyze a survey fielded by the Pew Research Center, a well-regarded nonpartisan survey organization, and released about a week before the 2016 presidential election (Pew Research Center 2016). The survey was conducted by telephone, with respondents sampled using RDD and then screened for eligibility among cell phone users. A total of 2,583 telephone interviews were completed, but after removing respondents who indicated that they would definitely not vote, we were left with a sample of 2,074 respondents. As the Pew dataset does not include design weights, we treat the survey as a **simple random sample (SRS)** from the universe of possible voters.

The outcome of interest in this survey is respondents' intended presidential vote, defined to include those who "leaned" towards one candidate. In the unweighted sample, 49.6% of respondents favored Clinton and 44.3% favored Trump. The survey thus gave Clinton a margin of 5.6% of the major-party vote (SE = 2.3%), which was more than 3 percentage points higher than her actual margin of 2.2% (the dashed line in Figure 4.1). The survey also contains data on five auxiliary variables: age, gender, race, region, and educational attainment. We recoded these variables into the categories shown in Table 4.1, the third column of which reports the variables' unweighted distribution in the Pew sample. Since these variables are at least somewhat predictive of nonresponse and vote choice, they are potentially useful for increasing the accuracy of the survey-based estimate.

### 4.1.2 Target Population and Auxiliary Information

As noted above, we define the target population as those who voted in the 2016 presidential election. In an actual forecast, the characteristics of this population would have to be estimated based on a likely-voter model and data from the voter file and surveys such as the **American Community Survey (ACS)**. Here, to simplify the analysis, we take advantage of the auxiliary information contained in the post-election wave of the 2016 **Cooperative Congressional Election Study (CCES)**. We assume that the set of CCES respondents who said they "definitely voted" in the 2016 general election is, once weighted by the CCES's own adjustment weights, a representative sample from the target population. In addition to having a much larger sample size than Pew (44,769 usable cases vs. 2,074), the CCES estimate of Clinton's popular vote margin is very close to the true margin, both nationally (Figure 4.1) and within each state.

The CCES contains data on each of the five auxiliary variables mentioned in Section 4.1.1: gender, age, race, region, and education. Pew and the CCES appear to define and code these variables identically. Nevertheless, marginal distributions of the auxiliary variables do exhibit some substantial differences between the two data sources, as Table 4.1 shows. Particularly concerning is that the Pew sample is younger than the CCES and more highly educated. Adjusting for these discrepancies may have a substantial effect on election forecasts.

### *4.1.3 Auxiliary Vector and Population Targets*

Even with just five auxiliary variables, we still face a number of important choices in deciding how exactly to calibrate the sample. One choice, which is relatively unimportant, is which distance metric to use. In this example, we use the chi-square distance, which results in **linear weighting**. By contrast, the choice of how to specify the auxiliary vector $z_i$ is typically much more consequential. As noted in Section 2.1, the effectiveness of a given specification of the auxiliary vector depends on how well it predicts both the outcome $y_i$ and the response probability $\rho_i$. If $y_i$ and $\rho_i$ depend on the interaction of two or more auxiliary variables, then ideally $z_i$ should include this interaction. In most survey samples, however, the inclusion of all important interactions, not to mention full poststratification, results in small or even empty cells. To avoid this, the survey analyst can either drop auxiliary variables, drop interactions among them, or coarsen the variables by collapsing categories.

Of the many possible specifications of the auxiliary vector and population targets, we compare the following four:

1. The *marginal* distributions of age, gender, race, and region.
2. The *marginal* distributions of age, gender, race, region, and education.

3. The *joint* distribution of age (coarsened), gender, race, region, and education (coarsened).
4. The *marginal* distributions of age, gender, and the interaction of race and region, with region further interacted with education among whites only.

Specification (1) provides a baseline for the impact of weighting when only basic demographic targets are used. In some scenarios, such as when auxiliary information is derived from a voter file, these may be the only auxiliary variables available. Specification (2) adds education, which we now know was a key variable missing from many 2016 election polls.

In contrast to the first two specifications, specification (3) contains the joint rather than marginal distributions of the auxiliary variables. This leads to poststratification, a special case of linear weighting. However, as commonly happens in poststratification, some of the 768 age-gender-race-region-education cells are empty in the Pew sample. We therefore coarsened both age and education by collapsing them into three-category variables.[23] Even so, there remained 265 empty cells, most with very small population sizes, which we forced the poststratification function to ignore.

Finally, specification (4) employs an alternative solution to the problem of empty cells. Rather than coarsening (or dropping) variables, it includes a mix of marginal and joint distributions. The interactions included are based on substantive knowledge of the survey outcome and nonresponse mechanism, some of which we learned only after the election. Post-election analyses have emphasized the distinctiveness of low-education whites, particularly in Midwestern states. We therefore weight white respondents by both education and region but weight non-white respondents by region only.

### 4.1.4 Comparison of Results

Calibrating the Pew sample to the four sets of population targets yields four different sets of weights (all normalized to have a mean of 1). The weights in set (1) are the least variable, with a **design effect due to weighting** ($\text{deff}_{\text{Kish}}$) of 1.1 and a maximum weight of 2. Sets (2), (3), and (4) have $\text{deff}_{\text{Kish}}$ values around 1.4 and maximums of 3, 3, and 8 respectively. These values of $\text{deff}_{\text{Kish}}$ are below the conventional threshold of 1.5 (see Section 2.4), and as we will see, the estimated variances of the weighted and unweighted samples differ even less than their $\text{deff}_{\text{Kish}}$ values would suggest.

[23] For age, we collapsed everyone under the age of fifty-one. For education, we collapsed everyone without a college degree into a "no college" category and everyone with an associate's or bachelor's degree into a "college" category. Other categories were left as listed in Table 4.1.

Set (2), which is calibrated to the full set of education categories, exhibits a distinctive feature of linear weighting: several of the respondents are assigned negative weights. Most of the negatively weighted respondents have postgraduate degrees, an attribute that is highly overrepresented in the unweighted Pew sample (see Table 4.1). Although negative weights pose no formal problems for calibration, they are often seen as undesirable for general dissemination because some estimators require positive weights. (If positive weights are required, **entropy weighting** should be used instead of linear weighting.)

As Table 4.1 indicates, weighting brings Pew sample into rough congruence with the auxiliary variables' marginal distributions in the CCES. In particular, the weighted samples are younger, more female, more black, and less educated, with two exceptions. Unsurprisingly, calibration using auxiliary vector (1), which does not include education, does not bring the Pew sample any closer to the CCES on this variable. In addition, due to the collapsing of categories and empty cells in the Pew sample, calibrating (i.e., poststratifying) using auxiliary vector (3) does not quite match the CCES targets, especially on age and education.

The estimates from the different weighting schemes are compared in Figure 4.1. The dashed line at 2.3% in this plot indicates Clinton's actual popular margin over Trump (as a percentage of the major-party vote). As noted in Section 4.1.2., the CCES estimate of 2.6% (SE = 0.7%) is very close to the true value. By contrast, the unweighted Pew estimate (Pew 0) of 5.6% (SE = 2.3%) overstates Clinton's support by 3.3 percentage points, though because it is much less precise its 95% confidence interval still includes the true value. The same cannot be said when the survey is weighted to match marginals other than education (Pew 1), which overestimates Clinton's margin by 10 points (SE = 2.2%). This illustrates the important point that if the auxiliary vector is not well chosen, weighting can increase rather than decrease bias. Contrary to its $\text{deff}_{\text{Kish}}$ value of 1.1, however, its estimated standard error suggests that weighting by set (1) actually decreases rather than increases variance.

As Figure 4.1 shows, the other three sets of weights (Pew 2, Pew 3, and Pew 4) yield much more accurate point estimates than non-education weights (Pew 1). All, however, improve only very slightly over the unweighted estimate (Pew 0), while also increasing the estimates' variance by a small amount (though not as much as their $\text{deff}_{\text{Kish}}$ values imply). Nor does including interactions in the auxiliary vector make much difference, as Pew 2, which is weighted marginal targets only, does about as well as Pew 3 and Pew 4. In sum, calibrating with an auxiliary vector that omits education increases bias markedly while including education - whether interacted with other variables or not - decreases bias, but only slightly.

**Table 4.1** Auxiliary variable distributions in the targets (CCES) and sample (Pew). Values indicate the percent of observations in the category. "Pew 0" = unweighted; "Pew 1" = calibrated to marginals other than education; "Pew 2" = calibrated to all marginals; "Pew 3" = (partially) poststratified; "Pew 4" = calibrated to mix of marginals and interactions, including region × education among whites.

| Margin | CCES | Pew 0 | Pew 1 | Pew 2 | Pew 3 | Pew 4 | Variable |
|---|---|---|---|---|---|---|---|
| 18 to 35 | 28.8 | 19 | 28.8 | 28.8 | 24.5 | 28.8 | age |
| 36 to 50 | 21.3 | 20.9 | 21.3 | 21.3 | 25.7 | 21.3 | age |
| 51 to 64 | 29.8 | 31.8 | 29.8 | 29.8 | 29.8 | 29.8 | age |
| 65+ | 20.1 | 28.4 | 20.1 | 20.1 | 20 | 20.1 | age |
| Female | 50.8 | 47.3 | 50.8 | 50.8 | 50.8 | 50.8 | female |
| Male | 49.2 | 52.7 | 49.2 | 49.2 | 49.2 | 49.2 | female |
| Black | 11.8 | 8.9 | 11.8 | 11.8 | 11.7 | 11.8 | race |
| Hispanic | 6.5 | 7.6 | 6.5 | 6.5 | 6.5 | 6.5 | race |
| Other | 6.8 | 7.1 | 6.8 | 6.8 | 6.8 | 6.8 | race |
| White | 74.9 | 76.4 | 74.9 | 74.9 | 75 | 74.9 | race |
| Midwest | 23.4 | 22.3 | 23.4 | 23.4 | 23.4 | 23.4 | region |
| Northeast | 19.7 | 18.2 | 19.7 | 19.7 | 19.7 | 19.7 | region |
| South | 35.5 | 37.9 | 35.5 | 35.5 | 35.5 | 35.5 | region |
| West | 21.4 | 21.6 | 21.4 | 21.4 | 21.4 | 21.4 | region |
| No HS | 6.8 | 2.8 | 2.5 | 6.8 | 3.6 | 5.8 | educ |
| High school graduate | 30.6 | 19.7 | 19.6 | 30.6 | 28.6 | 28.1 | educ |
| Some college | 23 | 15.7 | 15.9 | 23 | 23.3 | 21.9 | educ |
| 2-year | 10.6 | 11.3 | 11.4 | 10.6 | 9.3 | 11 | educ |
| 4-year | 18.7 | 28.6 | 28.9 | 18.7 | 22.7 | 21 | educ |
| Post-grad | 10.4 | 21.9 | 21.6 | 10.4 | 12.6 | 12.2 | educ |

## 4.2 Discussion

The analysis in this section has been unrealistic in the sense that it takes advantage of knowledge – specifically, that the undersampling of low-education whites caused surveys to underestimate Trump's support – that was not fully apparent when the survey in question was conducted. Nevertheless, it highlights several practical lessons for applied survey researchers. Most fundamentally, this example shows that even the highest-quality surveys, such as those conducted by Pew, can be improved with adjustment weighting, though gains may be limited. At the same time, the results for specification (1) show that weighting is by no means guaranteed to make estimates more accurate.

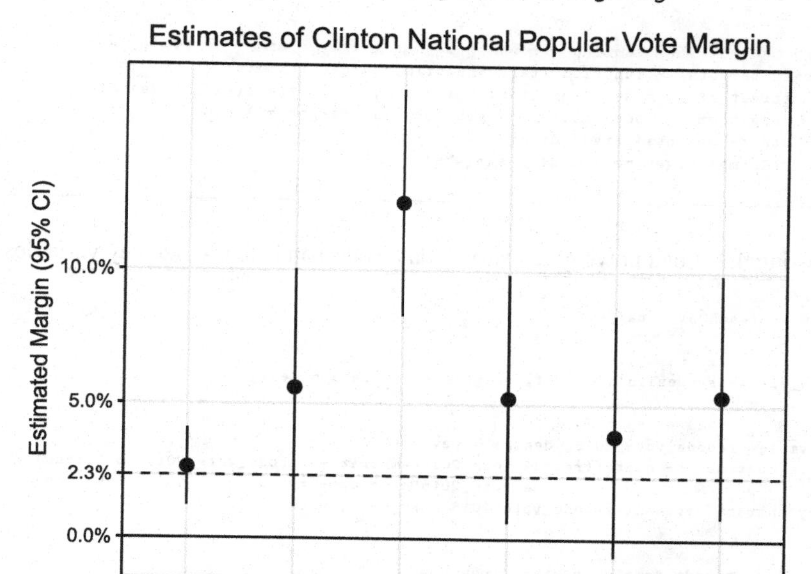


**Figure 4.1** Comparison of estimates for the 2016 US presidential election. Clinton's true margin over Trump is indicated by the dashed line at 2.3%. "CCES" = CCES estimate; "Pew 0" = unweighted; "Pew 1" = calibrated to marginals other than education; "Pew 2" = calibrated to all marginals; "Pew 3" = partially poststratified; "Pew 4" = calibrated to mix of marginals and interactions, including region × education among whites.

Successful weighting requires powerful auxiliary variables, in this case education. Getting the functional form of the relationships between these variables and $y$ and $\rho$ exactly right (i.e., by including the proper interactions), though in some contexts critical, is in this analysis a second-order concern. Finally, in some cases weighting slightly increased the estimators' variance. For all but specification (1), the reduction in bias more than compensated for the increased variance, but it is still worth noting that the differences in (squared) bias among the final three specifications pale relative to the variance of the estimates. There is, in short, only so much that can be learned from a survey sample of this size.

## 4.3 Example Code

The Code Ocean capsule for this section is published at `https://doi.org/10.24433/CO.0892243.v1`.

Listing 4.1 Setup

```
1 ### Packages
2 library(tidyverse)                    # for useful utilities
3 library(survey)                       # for analyzing complex surveys
4
```

```
5  ### Function for creating targets from auxiliary information and formula
6  create_targets <- function (target_design, target_formula) {
7      target_mf <- model.frame(target_formula, model.frame(target_design))
8      target_mm <- model.matrix(target_formula, target_mf)
9      wts <- weights(target_design)
10     colSums(target_mm * wts) / sum(wts)
11 }
```

Listing 4.2 Load unweighted survey data (Pew) and summarize key variables

```
1  ### Load
2  pew <- readRDS("data/pew.rds")
3
4  ### Make survey design
5  pew_srs <- svydesign(ids = ~1, weights = ~1, data = pew)
6
7  ### Unweighted survey estimates of presidential vote
8  svymean(~recode_vote_2016, design = pew_srs)
9  vote_contrast <- quote((recode_vote_2016Democrat - recode_vote_2016Republican) /
10                        (recode_vote_2016Democrat + recode_vote_2016Republican))
11 svycontrast(svymean(~recode_vote_2016, pew_srs), vote_contrast)
12
13 ### Auxiliary variables
14 svymean(~recode_female, design = pew_srs)
15 svymean(~recode_age_bucket, design = pew_srs)
16 svymean(~recode_race, design = pew_srs)
17 svymean(~recode_region, design = pew_srs)
18 svymean(~recode_educ, design = pew_srs)
```

Listing 4.3 Load auxiliary information (CCES) and summarize key variables

```
1  ### Load
2  cces <- readRDS("data/cces.rds")
3
4  ### Drop invalid cases
5  cces <- cces %>%
6      filter((CC16_401 == "I definitely voted in the General Election.") &
7             !is.na(commonweight_vv_post))
8
9  ### Make survey design
10 cces_awt <- svydesign(ids = ~1, weights = ~commonweight_vv_post, data = cces)
11
12 ### Presidential vote estimates
13 #### National
14 svymean(~recode_vote_2016, design = cces_awt, na.rm = TRUE)
15 svycontrast(svymean(~recode_vote_2016, cces_awt, na.rm = TRUE), vote_contrast)
16 #### State
17 svyby(~I(as.numeric(recode_vote_2016 == "Democrat")), ~recode_inputstate,
18       design = cces_awt, svymean, na.rm = TRUE, keep.var = FALSE)
19
20 ### Auxiliary variables
21 svymean(~recode_female, design = cces_awt)
22 svymean(~recode_age_bucket, design = cces_awt)
23 svymean(~recode_race, design = cces_awt)
24 svymean(~recode_region, design = cces_awt)
25 svymean(~recode_educ, design = cces_awt)
```

Listing 4.4 Create auxiliary vectors and population targets

```
1  ### Formulas for auxiliary vector
2
3  #### (1) Marginal distributions of age, female, race, and region
```

```
 4 formula_1 <- ~recode_age_bucket + recode_female + recode_race + recode_region
 5 #### (2) Marginal distributions of age, female, race, region, and education
 6 formula_2 <- ~recode_age_bucket + recode_female + recode_race + recode_region +
 7     recode_educ
 8 #### (3) Joint distribution of age (coarsened), female, race, region, and
 9 #### education (coarsened)
10 formula_3 <- ~recode_age_3way * recode_female * recode_race *
11     recode_region * recode_educ_3way
12 table(cces$recode_age_3way, cces$recode_age_bucket)
13 table(cces$recode_educ_3way, cces$recode_educ)
14 #### (4) Marginal distributions of age, female, and race and, among whites,
15 #### the joint distribution of region and education
16 #### (recode_race_educ_reg = race * educ * reg if race == "white" and
17 #### race * reg otherwise)
18 formula_4 <- ~recode_age_bucket + recode_female + recode_race_educ_reg
19
20 ### Population targets
21 targets_1 <- create_targets(cces_awt, formula_1)
22 targets_2 <- create_targets(cces_awt, formula_2)
23 targets_3 <- create_targets(cces_awt, formula_3) # will have to modify below
24 targets_4 <- create_targets(cces_awt, formula_4)
```

Listing 4.5 Create weighted survey designs

```
 1 #### (1)
 2 pew_lwt_1 <- calibrate(design = pew_srs,
 3                        formula = formula_1,
 4                        population = targets_1,
 5                        calfun = "linear")
 6
 7 #### (2)
 8 pew_lwt_2 <- calibrate(design = pew_srs,
 9                        formula = formula_2,
10                        population = targets_2,
11                        calfun = "linear")
12
13 #### (3)
14 ##### Can't compute below because some cells are empty.
15 try(pew_lwt_3 <- calibrate(design = pew_srs,
16                            formula = formula_3,
17                            population = targets_3,
18                            calfun = "linear"),
19     silent = TRUE)
20 ##### So instead we use the `postStratify` function with `partial = TRUE`, which
21 ##### ignores empty cells.
22 formula_3_ps <- as.formula(str_replace_all(formula_3, "\\*", "+"))
23 targets_3_ps <- svytable(formula = formula_3_ps, design = cces_awt)
24 sum(svytable(formula_3_ps, pew_srs) == 0) # 244 empty cells
25 pew_ps_3 <- postStratify(design = pew_srs,
26                          strata = formula_3_ps,
27                          population = targets_3_ps,
28                          partial = TRUE) # ignores empty cells
29
30 #### (4)
31 pew_lwt_4 <- calibrate(design = pew_srs,
32                        formula = formula_4,
33                        population = targets_4,
34                        calfun = "linear")
```

Listing 4.6 Examine weights

```
 1 #### Summarize and compare
 2 wts <- data.frame(wt1 = weights(pew_lwt_1) / mean(weights(pew_lwt_1)),
```

```
3                      wt2 = weights(pew_lwt_2) / mean(weights(pew_lwt_2)),
4                      wt3 = weights(pew_ps_3) / mean(weights(pew_ps_3)),
5                      wt4 = weights(pew_lwt_4) / mean(weights(pew_lwt_4)))
6
7  sapply(wts, summary)                      # ave(wts) = 1
8  sapply(wts, var)                          # Kish deff = 1 + var(wts) / ave(wts)^2
9
10 #### Boxplots
11 wts %>%
12     pivot_longer(everything()) %>%
13     ggplot(aes(x = name, y = value)) +
14     geom_boxplot()
15
16 #### Negative weights
17 pew_lwt_2$variables %>%
18     filter(weights(pew_lwt_2) < 0) %>%
19     group_by(recode_race_educ) %>%
20     summarise(count = n())
21 pew_lwt_4$variables %>%
22     filter(weights(pew_lwt_4) < 0) %>%
23     group_by(recode_race_educ) %>%
24     summarise(count = n())
```

Listing 4.7 Compare marginal distributions of auxiliary variables

```
1  aux_comp <- data.frame(
2      cces = svymean(formula_2, design = cces_awt),
3      pew0 = svymean(formula_2, design = pew_srs),
4      pew1 = svymean(formula_2, design = pew_lwt_1),
5      pew2 = svymean(formula_2, design = pew_lwt_2),
6      pew3 = svymean(formula_2, design = pew_ps_3),
7      pew4 = svymean(formula_2, design = pew_lwt_4))
8  print(aux_comp, digits = 2)
```

Listing 4.8 Compare estimates of Clinton-Trump margin

```
1  ### Actual results
2  pres <- readRDS("data/election.rds")
3
4  natl_margin <- pres %>%
5      summarise(margin = (sum(demtotal) - sum(reptotal)) /
6                   (sum(demtotal) + sum(reptotal))) %>%
7      as.numeric()
8  natl_margin
9
10 ### Compare estimates
11 comp_df <- data.frame(
12     CCES = svycontrast(svymean(~recode_vote_2016, cces_awt, na.rm = TRUE),
13                        vote_contrast),
14     Pew_0 = svycontrast(svymean(~recode_vote_2016, pew_srs, na.rm = TRUE),
15                        vote_contrast),
16     Pew_1 = svycontrast(svymean(~recode_vote_2016, pew_lwt_1, na.rm = TRUE),
17                        vote_contrast),
18     Pew_2 = svycontrast(svymean(~recode_vote_2016, pew_lwt_2, na.rm = TRUE),
19                        vote_contrast),
20     Pew_3 = svycontrast(svymean(~recode_vote_2016, pew_ps_3, na.rm = TRUE),
21                        vote_contrast),
22     Pew_4 = svycontrast(svymean(~recode_vote_2016, pew_lwt_4, na.rm = TRUE),
23                        vote_contrast)) %>%
24     pivot_longer(cols = everything(),
25                  names_to = c("source", ".value"),
26                  names_pattern = "(.*)\\.(.*)") %>%
27     rename(est = nlcon) %>%
```

```
28      mutate(err = est - natl_margin,
29             source = str_replace(source, "_", " "))
30  comp_df
```

## 5 Application to Quota-Sampled Opinion Polls

In the mid-1930s, George Gallup, Elmo Roper, and other pioneering pollsters began surveying the American public on a regular basis. By the time University of Michigan researchers fielded the first full-scale national election study in 1952, nonacademic survey organizations had conducted some 500 national polls, nearly all of which have been archived by the Roper Center for Public Opinion Research (`https://ropercenter.cornell.edu`). The majority of the archived polls were conducted by Gallup's **American Institute of Public Opinion (AIPO)**, but the archive also includes numerous polls by the three other major survey organizations of this era: Roper's eponymous firm, Hadley Cantril's **Office of Public Opinion Research (OPOR)**, and the **National Opinion Research Council (NORC)**. These survey data contain a treasure trove of information on the attitudes of the American public during a critical era that stretched from the waning years of the Great Depression to the first stirrings of the civil rights movement.

Yet despite its value, this unique data source has remained largely untapped by political scientists and other scholars, primarily because analyzing the data is far from straightforward. Though archived by the Roper Center, many of the raw datasets were not touched for decades and are difficult to read and manipulate. As a consequence, the individual-level data were mostly ignored by scholars for many years.[24] Recently, however, Adam Berinsky and Eric Schickler, with funding from the National Science Foundation, have led a collaborative effort with the Roper Center to organize, recode, and archive the polls into usable datasets (Berinsky and Schickler 2011). Transforming the data into a suitable format is only half the battle, however; a second barrier to their widespread use is that the poll samples themselves are not representative of the American public.

This unrepresentativeness stems from two sources, one intentional and one unintentional. First, since the purpose of many of the polls was predicting elections, the poll samples were often intended to be representative of *voters*, not the public at large. Second, only after the polling debacle of the 1948 election did survey firms begin gradually transitioning to **probability sampling** (Mosteller

[24] Exceptions to this neglect include Verba and Schlozman (1977), Caldeira (1987), Weatherford and Sergeyev (2000), Baum and Kernell (2001).

et al. 1949), a process essentially complete by 1952. Before then, all commercial polls selected survey respondents purposively using **quota sampling**. Quota-controlled samples are designed to be representative of the target population on certain observable characteristics, but because interviewers exercise discretion over whom to interview within quota categories, there is no guarantee that the resulting samples will be representative on noncontrolled attributes. As a result of these two sources of unrepresentativeness, poll samples before the 1950s exhibited marked racial, class, regional, and gender biases relative to the American public (Berinsky 2006).

To address these biases, Berinsky (2006) proposed weighting samples to match known population targets, an approach implemented by Berinsky et al. (2011) for polls conducted between 1936 and 1945. The weights created by this team were a marked improvement over the raw samples, but they nevertheless had several shortcomings. Owing to the limitations of the population data collected by Berinsky et al. and of the weighting methodology they employed, the weights they created did not make optimal use of all auxiliary information. In particular, the weights were based on static population data from only a single census (1940). Further, because Berinsky et al. relied mainly on poststratification, they could not incorporate all auxiliary variables into a given set of weights. They thus instead created separate weight sets based, respectively, on occupation, education, and phone ownership.

In this section, we describe a new approach to weighting quota-sampled polls that improves on that of Berinsky et al. in four main respects. First, whereas the Berinsky et al. weights extend only through 1945, our weights cover the entire 1936–1952 period, thus fully bridging the gap between the eras of quota sampling and probability sampling. Second, the weights we create are dynamic rather than static, in that they are designed to yield samples representative of the US population as it evolved over this period. Third, at each point in time we rely on more accurate and detailed auxiliary information on the US population, incorporating demographic variables beyond those used by Berinsky et al. and more detailed information on the joint distribution of those variables. Fourth, we use a more flexible weighting method, calibration weighting, a generalization of better-known techniques like poststratification that enables us to make more efficient use of auxiliary information. Using this improved methodology, we create weights that not only cover nearly every public opinion poll conducted between 1936 and the first quarter of 1953 but also are more effective than the existing weights at reducing the sampling and nonresponse biases in the raw poll samples. While no panacea for the issues inherent in nonprobability samples, these weights nevertheless enable scholars to make more credible inferences about public opinion in a critical era before the adoption of probability sampling.

## 5.1 Auxiliary Variables and Dynamic Population Targets

The key to reducing nonresponse bias is to take advantage of auxiliary information on survey variables' distribution in the population of interest, by collecting more comprehensive and accurate information than previously available on the evolving composition of the US adult population. We did so by, first, collecting population data on additional auxiliary variables beyond those Berinsky et al. (2011) used to create weights for polls conducted in 1936–1945. Second, whereas Berinsky et al.'s weights were based on only a single US Census (1940), our new weights take advantage of data collected at many points in time. With a specially developed interpolation model, we used these data to estimate the demographic composition of the US population in each year between 1936 and 1953. These detailed demographic snapshots of the United States provided the population targets we then used to generate survey weights for each poll.

The auxiliary variables Berinsky et al. used to create weights for the 1936–1945 polls were *Region*, *Black*, *Female*, and one of either *Education*, *Professional*, or *Phone*. Except for phone ownership, which was calculated from AT&T corporate records, the population targets for these variables were derived from **Integrated Public Use Microdata Series (IPUMS)** samples of the 1940 US Census (Ruggles et al. 2010). To create our revised weights, we collected population data on four additional auxiliary variables – *State*, *Farm*, *Urban*, and *Age* – and did so across multiple years. Gathering population data for various points in time is important, especially given our longer time span, because in some respects the demographic composition of the United States changed markedly over this period. The percentage of American adults with no more than a grade school education, for example, fell from 60% in 1936 to 45% in 1952. There was also substantial change in the joint distribution of certain demographic variables, such as *Black* and *Region*. In 1936, for example, only 33% of African Americans lived outside the former Confederacy, but by 1952 fully 44% did. Incorporating such changes into our targets helps ensure that the weighted samples accurately reflect the evolving demographic composition of the US public.

Table 5.1 describes the nine auxiliary variables we used to create the new weights. The column labeled "Type" indicates each variable's role in the sampling scheme used by Gallup's AIPO. (Polls conducted by other organizations generally included a subset of these variables.) As Berinsky (2006)

**Table 5.1** Auxiliary variables.

| Name | Levels | Type | Source of Population Data |
|---|---|---|---|
| *State* | lower-48 states | central | IPUMS (1930, 1940, 1950, 1960) |
| *Farm* | non-farm/farm | central | IPUMS (1930, 1940, 1950, 1960) |
| *Urban* | rural/urban | central | IPUMS (1930, 1940),<br>census reports (1950, 1960) |
| *Female* | male/female | hard quota | IPUMS (1930, 1940, 1950, 1960) |
| *Age* | 21–34/35–49/50+ | soft quota | IPUMS (1930, 1940, 1950, 1960) |
| *Professional* | non-prof./prof. | soft quota | IPUMS (1930, 1940, 1950, 1960) |
| *Black* | non-black/black | implicit quota | IPUMS (1930, 1940, 1950, 1960) |
| *Education* | elem./some HS/<br>HS grad/college+ | no quota | IPUMS (1940, 1960),<br>retrospective extrapolation (HS 1930) |
| *Phone* | no phone/phone | no quota | IPUMS (1960),<br>AT&T (1930, 1935, 1937, 1940, 1945),<br>*Hist. Stats. of U.S.* (1936–1953) |

describes, the sample distributions of the variables *State*, *Farm*, and *Urban* were determined by the AIPO central office's purposive selection of interviewing locations. AIPO interviewers were given a hard quota for the gender breakdown in their sample, while for *Age* and *Professional* they were encouraged but not required to get "a good spread." A similarly soft, if less explicit, quota was imposed for black respondents, who especially in the South were interviewed only "as encountered," which is to say, rarely. Aside from a general admonition to distribute their interviews across class lines, there was no quota for *Education* or *Phone*, both strong markers of socioeconomic status. Except for *Education*, which first becomes available in 1943, all of these variables were included in the vast majority of AIPO surveys.

As Table 5.1 indicates, data on the population distributions of the auxiliary variables must be derived from a variety of sources. The most important of these data sources are IPUMS samples of individual-level US census records, which are especially useful because they (unlike aggregate census reports) reveal the joint distribution of the auxiliary variables. Unfortunately, the IPUMS datasets do not include every census variable in every year. For privacy reasons, the 1950 and 1960 IPUMS samples do not include *Urban*, so for these years we must rely on US census reports on urban population by state. Similarly, *Education* is only available in the 1940 and 1960 IPUMS. To establish educational trends before 1940, we rely on Folger and Nam (1964), who estimate the national proportion of high school graduates in 1930 by extrapolating backward from later censuses.

The US Census did not ask about telephone ownership until 1960, so only in that year are data available on its joint distribution with other variables. The AT&T corporate archives, however, contain information on the number of residential telephone lines in each state for several years between 1930 and 1945.

The census also estimated the proportion of households in the United States with a telephone in each year during this period, figures reported in *Historical Statistics of the United States* (Field 2006). By combining all of this information with (interpolated) decennial census data on the number of households in each state, we derived state-level estimates of the proportion of citizens with a phone in their household.

These raw data provide a rich but incomplete picture of the US population. Most obviously, the data are available only every few (usually ten) years. Targets for intervening years must therefore be estimated based on some model of demographic change. If data on the full joint distribution of auxiliary variables were available in each census year, cell proportions in the intervening years could be estimated through a simple interpolation model. Enns and Koch (2013), for example, construct annual population targets for the years 1950–2000 by linearly interpolating between the cell proportions in each decadal IPUMS sample. Unfortunately, such a simple approach is not possible in our case because IPUMS samples in different years include different sets of auxiliary variables.

Nor would it be acceptable in this application to simply interpolate auxiliary variables' *marginal* distributions and then construct raking weights to match the margins in each year. This application poses two related barriers to raking on marginals only. First, matching the marginal population distribution of each variable does not address nonresponse bias that results from the interaction of two or more variables. An example of such an interaction is Gallup's tendency to over-sample citizens who were both phone owners and professionals. Because response probabilities depended on the interaction of *Phone* and *Professional*, Gallup polls weighted to match the marginal distributions of *Phone* and *Professional* still tend to overestimate the phone ownership rate among professionals by about 15 percentage points.

A second, more obvious problem with weighting to match marginal distributions only is that many polls from this period excluded Southern blacks entirely. Thus, for these polls we must change the target population from the US **voting-age population (VAP)** to the subpopulation of all adults except Southern blacks. We refer to the latter subpopulation as the de facto **voting-eligible population (VEP)** – that is, the subset of American adults who could potentially vote – in reference to the fact that African Americans were effectively disenfranchised in the former Confederacy at this time.[25] We note, however, that

[25] Although African Americans were legally entitled to vote under the Fifteenth Amendment, the states of the former Confederacy used a variety of legal and extra-legal mechanisms to effectively disfranchise their black citizens. There is no perfect dividing line between states

constitutionally speaking Southern blacks were entitled to vote, and thus the label "voting-eligible public" may suggest an overly rigid distinction between the eligible electorate and the public as a whole.

It should be emphasized that simply changing the marginal targets for *Black* would not adequately account for this change in the target population from the VAP to the VEP. The targets for other auxiliary variables correlated with *Black* must be changed as well, which requires knowing their joint distribution with *Black*. For variables available in every IPUMS sample, the joint distribution can be estimated by interpolating the cell proportions between census years, but such a simple approach will not work for variables such as *Phone*, whose joint distribution with most variables is known only for 1960.

This problem, which was illustrated in simple form in Section 3.1, is present on a larger and more complex scale when we consider all nine auxiliary variables in Table 5.1. To address this problem comprehensively, we rely on the dynamic **ecological inference (EI)** framework developed by Caughey and Wang (2019).[26] Our goal is to estimate the yearly population proportions of all 27,648 cells defined by the complete cross-classification of the auxiliary variables in Table 5.1.[27] If we considered each year separately, we would face the usual ecological inference problem that the interior cells cannot be estimated without strong and often unwarranted modeling assumptions. A distinctive feature of our application, however, is the availability of rich multivariate data at a few points in time (i.e., census years). Assuming that variables' conditional joint distribution changes gradually over time, we can use years with a lot of data to inform estimates for years with less data (or none at all).

As Section 3.3 discusses, Caughey and Wang's approach uses a Bayesian framework that combines a sampling model for the observed marginal data

---

where blacks could and could not vote, especially since black political mobilization increased markedly over this period. Based on our reading of the scholarly literature, we believe that the most principled division is between the former Confederacy – where black voting was negligible before 1944 – and the rest of the nation (following, e.g., Key 1949; Mickey 2015). Kentucky, though classified as Southern by Gallup, did not substantially restrict black voting. The same appears to hold, though less certainly, for Oklahoma, at least by the late 1930s (Bunche 1973).

26 For further details, see Caughey and Wang (2014).

27 Since there are extremely few farms in urban areas, we collapse *Farm* and *Urban* into a new variable, *Size*, with three levels: farm, rural non-farm, and urban. This results in $48 \times 3 \times 2 \times 3 \times 2 \times 2 \times 4 \times 2 = 27{,}648$ cells. To reduce the computational burden we estimated the cell proportions in three stages and combined the estimates together. In the first stage, we estimated the yearly population proportions of groups defined by the interaction of all the variables in Table 5.1 except *State*, which was replaced by *South*. In the second stage, we did the same at the state level but excluded *Education* and *Age*. The two sets of estimates were combined by raking the full cell matrix to match both sets of partial estimates.

with a transition model for the cell proportions' temporal evolution. The estimated cell proportions in a given year are informed both by data from that year (if any) and by cell estimates from other years. The cell estimates satisfy known constraints – for example, that in a given year the proportion of Southern blacks with a phone plus the proportion of Southern blacks without a phone must equal the observed proportion of Southern blacks; but within these constraints, the cell estimates are also influenced by information from other years – for example, the negative correlation between *Black* and *Phone* in the 1960 IPUMS data. In this sense, the Caughey-Wang model uses all available information to inform estimates of the demographic composition of the population at each point in time.

The dynamic EI model yields estimates of the population proportions of 27,648 demographic types in each year between 1930 and 1960. From this estimate of $f_{\mathcal{U}}(\boldsymbol{x})$, we can derive any population targets of interest, whether they be marginal distributions (e.g., the proportion in each region) or joint distributions (e.g., the proportion of urban residents in each education category). As we describe in the following section, these targets can then be used to create weights that ensure that survey samples match the specified population moments.

## 5.2 Creating Survey Weights

Before we can create weights, we need to specify an auxiliary vector $\boldsymbol{z}_i$ and corresponding population targets $\tilde{T}_{\boldsymbol{x}}$. Our selection of auxiliary vector relies on a combination of background knowledge of the sampling process, statistical analysis of survey outcomes and nonresponse, and consideration of the important subpopulations. We know that intentional and unintentional biases led polling organizations to undersample women, Southerners, African Americans (especially in the South), and lower-class individuals. Statistical analyses of response probabilities helped refine our understanding of the nonresponse mechanism. We found, for example, that surveys undersampled women less in the South than in the non-South and that the gender gap in voter turnout was larger in the South. In other words, both nonresponse and turnout (a likely outcome variable) depended on the interaction of region and gender. We therefore made sure that the auxiliary vector included this interaction as well as others we detected. Finally, since we anticipated that many users would be interested in examining subpopulations defined by gender, class, and region, we prioritized interactions that define these domains of interest. Of course, the feasibility of including these interactions was limited by the poll samples themselves:

If no sampled individuals exhibited a given combination of attributes (e.g., black female farmer), then it was impossible to construct weights that match the population in this respect. The weights we ultimately created reflect our attempts to balance these various considerations.

We aimed to create general-purpose weights that applied analysts could use for a wide variety of research questions, while also recognizing that the "best" set of weights always depends on the goal of the analysis. We therefore created four main sets of weights, which differ from each other in two respects: (1) the target population to which they are calibrated and (2) the auxiliary vector on which they are based. Since poll samples differ systematically across AIPO, OPOR, and NORC, we also tailored our weighting schemes to each survey organization. The weight sets are summarized in Table 5.2.

The first way that the weights differ is with respect to their target population. For AIPO polls, the distinction is between weights calibrated to the *voting-age* population (VAP) of all US adults over the age of twenty-one or to the *voting-eligible* population (VEP) of all US adults except African Americans in the former Confederacy. This distinction between VAP and VEP is a practical concession to the fact that Gallup, aiming to produce samples representative of the active electorate, undersampled Southern blacks so severely that in many polls they are missing entirely. Since the VAP weights do not (and typically cannot) interact *South* and *Black*, they implicitly allow non-Southern blacks to "stand in" for the absent Southern blacks in estimates of national opinion.[28] The VEP weights avoid this assumption and are also typically less variable than the VAP weights but at the expense of changing the population about which inferences can be made. The problem of empty cells is even more extreme in OPOR and NORC polls; moreover, these polls did not record respondents' state of residence. For these reasons, for these polls we created *white public* weights that drop all blacks from the target population. For OPOR polls, we created white public and VEP weights, and for NORC polls we created white public and VAP weights.

In addition to differing with respect to target population, alternative weighting sets also differed in the auxiliary vector used to calibrate them. What we label "comparable" weights are based on the subset of auxiliary variables included in nearly all Gallup polls: *Phone*, *Female*, *Region*, *Professional*, *Black*, and *Size* (a combination of *Farm* and *Urban*). Because they are based on a single consistent auxiliary vector, the comparable weights ensure that

[28] For evidence that this is often a reasonable assumption, see Schickler and Caughey (2011). To avoid extreme weights, we do not create VAP weights for polls with fewer than twenty black respondents.

differences in estimates across polls are not the result of differences in the weighting scheme.[29] Although the comparable weights substantially increase the representativeness of the poll samples (see Section 5.3), weights based on *Education* do so even more effectively. Thus, for the approximately half of Gallup polls that include this variable, all of which were fielded after 1942, we also created "education" weights based on an auxiliary vector that includes not only the variables used to create the comparable weights but also *Education* and *Age*.[30] Finally, for the relatively few polls with missing cells or auxiliary variables, we still create the "best feasible" weights for that poll, except for a few cases where it was impossible to create any weights at all. Unlike the comparable and education weights, the best feasible weights are based on a different auxiliary vector in every poll (and thus are not summarized in Table 5.2).

For applied users, choosing which weights to use will often entail a trade-off between maximizing comparability over time and reducing bias in a given poll as much as possible. For most analyses, education weights will be the best choice because they are the most effective at reducing the class bias in the poll samples. However, if education weights are not available in a given poll, or if one desires comparability with polls without education weights (e.g., for over-time analyses), then comparable weights should be used instead. Only when both comparable and education weights are unavailable should one rely on the best feasible weights, which are neither as comparable across polls nor as effective at reducing bias as the other weights.

Researchers should also carefully consider their population of interest. If they wish to make inferences about the US public as a whole, then they should use weights calibrated to that target population (e.g., `WtPubComp` or `WtPubEd`). On the other hand, if they are interested in the eligible electorate (that is, excluding disfranchised Southern blacks), then VEP weights are preferable. Similarly, if one wishes to examine subpopulations defined by some variable, it is best to use weights that calibrate the interaction of that variable with all others (see column 6 of Table 5.2). For example, if one is interested in estimating public opinion in the non-South, one should use `WtVotEd` rather than `WtPubEd` because the former ensures that all other auxiliary variables are calibrated within values of *South*.

[29] Of course, even with the auxiliary vector held constant, differences in estimates across polls could reflect differences in the sampling process and/or nonresponse mechanism rather than true changes in the population.

[30] The education weights for NORC polls do not use *Age* as an auxiliary variable. Also, of the more than 200 polls that contained *Education*, 24 could not be weighted using the auxiliary vector summarized in Table 5.2. We continue to use the "Ed" suffix for these weight variables, but we include a flag in the documentation for these polls indicating that their auxiliary vector is not strictly identical to that of other education weights.

**Table 5.2** Summary of survey weights.

| Org. | Weight Name | Pop. | Weight Type | Auxiliary Variables | Interacted Variables | % Wtd. |
|---|---|---|---|---|---|---|
| AIPO | WtPubComp | Adults | Comparable | Phone, Professional, Female, Region, South, Black, Size | Phone, Female | 91% |
| ⋮ | WtVotComp | Voters | Comparable | Phone, Professional, Female, Region, South, Black, Size | Phone, Female, South | 91% |
| ⋮ | WtPubEd | Adults | Education | Phone, Professional, Female, Region, South, Black, Size, Education, Age | Phone, Female, Education | 46% |
| ⋮ | WtVotEd | Voters | Education | Phone, Professional, Female, Region, South, Black, Size, Education, Age | Phone, Female, South, Education | 45% |
| OPOR | WtVotComp | Voters | Comparable | Phone, Professional, Female, Region, South, Black, Size, Age | South | 76% |
| ⋮ | WtWhtComp | Whites | Comparable | Phone, Professional, Female, Region, South, Size, Age | Phone, Female, South | 100% |
| ⋮ | WtVotEd | Voters | Education | Phone, Professional, Female, Region, South, Black, Size, Education, Age | South | 76% |
| ⋮ | WtWhtEd | Whites | Education | Phone, Professional, Female, Region, South, Size, Education, Age | Phone, Female, South, Education | 100% |
| NORC | WtPubEd | Adults | Education | Female, Black, South, Size, Education | Female, Education | 100% |
| ⋮ | WtWhtEd | Whites | Education | Female, South, Size, Education | Female, South, Education | 100% |

**Table 5.3** Population benchmarks and sample estimates (%).

| | Car (1948) | Some High Sch+ | Some College+ | Turnout | Republican |
|---|---|---|---|---|---|
| Unweighted | 54.6 | 65.8 | 23.0 | 78.5 | 52.3 |
| Comp Wts | 51.9 | 62.9 | 20.4 | 75.3 | 49.2 |
| Benchmark | 49.4 | 49.5 | 12.4 | 56.4 | 48.4 |

## 5.3 Validation

The purpose of the weights we have created is to improve the representativeness of the poll samples. By construction, the weights will succeed in doing so on auxiliary variables used to create the weights in the first place: *Professional*, *Female*, *Black*, and so on. The real test of their performance, however, is their ability to improve representativeness with respect to demographic and political characteristics *not* used to create the weights. Moreover, the new weights should improve representativeness not only relative to the unweighted samples but also relative to the weights initially devised by Berinsky et al. (2011), which incorporated less auxiliary information.

In this section, we validate the new comparable weights' performance by evaluating their ability to match five population benchmarks. The first of these benchmarks is the percentage of adults who owned an automobile, which we derived from a probability-sampled survey of consumer finances fielded in 1948 by the University of Michigan's **Survey Research Center (SRC).**[31] The second and third benchmarks are the percentages of adults who had attended, respectively, at least some high school and at least some college (education weights, of course, match the benchmarks exactly). The fourth benchmark is voter turnout, operationalized as the number of votes cast in the previous presidential election as a percentage of the VAP. The fifth is the Republican percentage of the two-party vote in the succeeding presidential election. We compare these benchmarks to survey estimates derived from questions on car ownership, education level, retrospective voting, and prospective vote intention.

As a first cut, Table 5.3 compares unweighted and weighted sample estimates to population benchmarks, averaging across all polls that included the benchmark variable for which comparable weights can be calculated.[32] All of the

[31] Economic Behavior Program, Survey Research Center, University of Michigan. 1948.

[32] To ensure that these summary statistics are based on comparable samples, Table 5.3 does not include estimates using the Berinsky-Schickler weights, which are not available for

weighted estimates are calculated using comparable VAP weights except the Republican estimate, which is based on comparable VEP weights. The table makes two patterns clear. First, consistent with the socioeconomic bias in the quota samples, the unweighted survey percentages are higher on average than the corresponding population benchmarks. In the case of car ownership and Republican presidential vote intention (columns 1 and 5), the unweighted estimates are only 4–5 percentage points off. The biases for education and voter turnout, however, are 2–4 times larger.[33] Second, Table 5.3 also indicates that weighting improves the accuracy of sample estimates for all five benchmark variables, reducing the difference in averages on each variable by 3–4 percentage points. In the case of car ownership and Republican vote intention, this is sufficient to nearly eliminate the bias in the poll samples.[34] For the other three variables, however, the new weights only eliminate a fraction of the bias. This underscores the value of using education weights, which for comparability were not used in this validation exercise, in the subset of polls that measured respondents' education level.

While it is reassuring that our new weights improve the representativeness of the raw poll samples, a more stringent test is whether they improve on the weights that Berinsky et al. (2011) created for polls fielded between 1936 and 1945. To evaluate this, we compare how close the new weights, old weights, and unweighted samples get to population benchmarks for the variables examined in Table 5.3. For every variable except car ownership, we make these comparisons for both the voting-age and voting-eligible population, using the appropriate weights and benchmarks for each.[35] The polls used in each comparison vary depending on the availability of the relevant benchmarks, survey variables, and weights.

---

polls after 1945. Figure 5.1, which compares estimates within each poll, does include the Berinsky-Schickler weights.

33 The bias in turnout, which is based on respondents' self-report of whether they voted in the last presidential election, almost certainly reflects over-reporting as well as sample selection bias. Indeed, biases of similar magnitude can be found in probability samples such as the American National Elections Study (Ansolabehere and Hersh 2012, 446).

34 If, instead, VAP rather than VEP weights are used to estimate prospective Republican vote, the weighted estimates slightly overshoot the benchmark, averaging 1.4% under the ultimate Republican percentage.

35 The "new weights" used in this comparison were the comparable weights for the voting-age and voting-eligible publics (`WtPubComp` and `WtVotComp`, respectively). The corresponding "old weights" were cell weights based on the auxiliary variables *Professional*, *Black*, *Female*, and *South*. Voter turnout in the voting-eligible population was calculated by dividing VAP turnout by the proportion of US adults who were not Southern blacks. For both the VAP and the VEP, the benchmark for Republican vote intention was the Republican candidate's actual two-party share in the next presidential election.

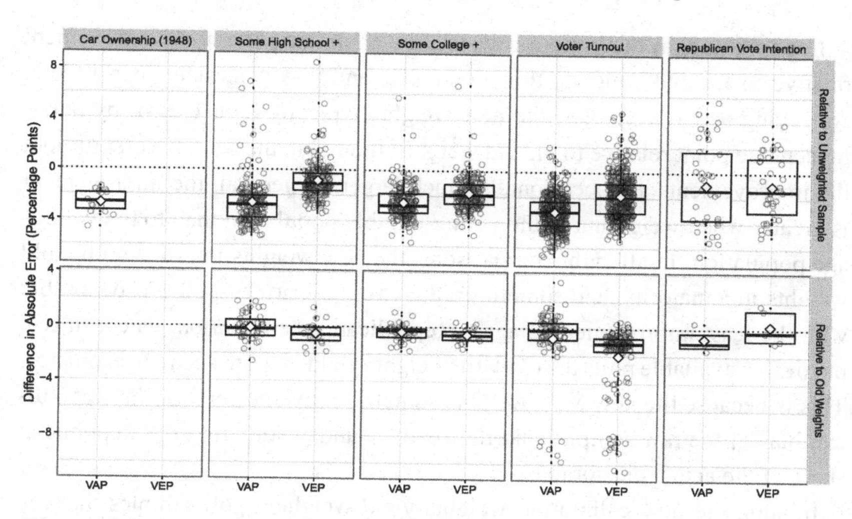


**Figure 5.1** Improvement in matching out-of-sample benchmarks using the new weights. Values less than 0 (dotted line) indicate that the new weights improved the accuracy of estimates. The top row of panels compares the new weights to the unweighted poll samples, and the bottom row compares the new weights to the old weights. Each column corresponds to a different population benchmark, for the voting-age population (VAP) and the voting-eligible population (VEP, i.e., excluding Southern blacks). Circles represent poll-specific differences in absolute error between the new weights and either the unweighted samples or the old weights. Absolute error is the absolute value of the difference between the population benchmark (e.g., the percentage of adults who owned a car) and the corresponding sample estimate. Diamonds indicate the average difference in absolute error, and the box plots overlaid over the points indicate medians and interquartile intervals.

Figure 5.1 plots the results of these comparisons. The panels in the top row compare the new weights and unweighted samples in terms of **difference in absolute error (DAE)**, and the bottom row does the same for the new weights and old weights. In addition to plotting the DAE of each poll, the figure also indicates the average DAE across polls as well as the 25th, 50th, and 75th percentiles. Corroborating Table 5.3, the top row of Figure 5.1 indicates that in a large majority of polls, using the new weights yields estimates closer to the benchmarks than the unweighted estimates. The median reduction in error across benchmarks ranges between 1 and 3 percentage points. The improvement is least consistent for Republican vote intention, which is unsurprising since most of the poll samples were specifically designed for the purpose of predicting election outcomes. In almost every case where the unweighted estimate was closer to the benchmark, the new weights underpredicted Republican vote share, an outcome to be expected if (as was probably the case) voters leaned Republican relative to nonvoters.

Looking now at the bottom row, we see a similar pattern of improvement relative to the old weights, though smaller and less consistent than before. Averaging across variables, the new weights typically reduce error by half a percentage point relative to the old weights, though in the case of voter turnout the improvements are occasionally much larger. In general, the improvement is greater when weighting to the voting-eligible population than to the voting-age population. In all eight comparisons, the new weights improve on the old weights in a majority, and sometimes the vast majority, of polls. The variable with the least improvement is again Republican vote intention, where in two out of five available polls the old VEP weights yielded more accurate estimates. This is because the new VEP weights sometimes overcorrect for the Republican bias in the raw samples and thus end up underestimating the Republican share of the actual electorate.

In sum, the new calibration weights yield weighted poll samples that are much more representative of the target population than the unweighted samples, and for some variables the weighted samples recover external benchmarks almost exactly. The new weights also generally improve over the Berinsky et al. (2011) weights, which incorporated less auxiliary information (and are available only through 1945). Evaluating the new weights against external benchmarks thus provides compelling validation of their effectiveness at improving the representativeness of the poll samples. It should be emphasized that the comparable weights do not incorporate information on education, the most powerful indicator of socioeconomic status in the polls. The upper-class bias in the unweighted samples can be further reduced by using education weights in the polls for which these weights are available, a fact we illustrate in the following section.

## 5.4 Macropartisanship, 1937–1953

To illustrate the substantive consequences of weighting, we compare weighted and unweighted trends in party identification between 1937 and 1953, replicating a similar analysis by Norpoth, Sidman, and Suong (2013). Using the unweighted poll samples,[36] Norpoth et al. find that Democratic identification declined dramatically in the late 1930s and early 1940s, even falling below Republican identification in the mid-1940s. Only during the 1948 election campaign, they argue, did "the Democratic lead in party identification reach . . .

[36] These authors did not use weights because they concluded that the weights then available for polls before 1946 did not significantly increase the estimated share of Democratic identifiers (Norpoth, Sidman, and Suong 2013, 151, n 6).

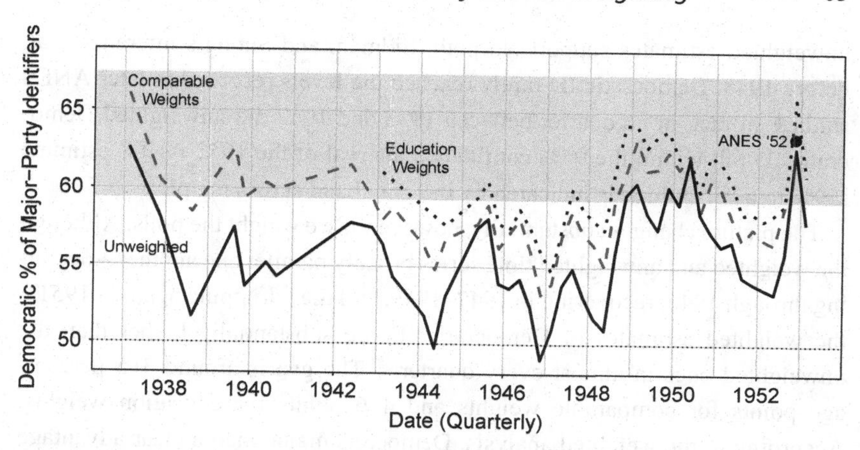


**Figure 5.2** Weighted and unweighted trends in party identification in the US public, 1937–1953. The solid line tracks the unweighted quarterly percentage of Democrats among major-party identifiers. The dashed and dotted lines track the same quantity estimated using comparable and education weights, respectively. The dot labeled "ANES '52" is the Democratic percentage in the 1952 ANES study, and the gray band is the estimate's 95% confidence interval. Note that comparable weights are not available after the third quarter of 1952.

the magnitude that would be recorded in the National Election Studies for decades to come" (p. 147). In their view, this evidence suggests that it was the Democrats' successful management of the Second World War and the post-war economy, not the economic crisis and policy innovations of the 1930s, that gave the party a durable majority in the American public.

We explore whether using our new weights alters these conclusions. To do so, we first calculated the weighted and unweighted Democratic percentage of major-party identifiers (that is, Democrats and Republicans) in each of the 166 polls that contain a party ID question and appropriate weights. We then averaged polls within quarters, yielding a quarterly time-series of the percent Democratic among party identifiers that is analogous to the "macropartisanship" series created by Mackuen, Erikson, and Stimson (1989) for the post-1945 period. Figure 5.2 plots the quarterly estimates for the unweighted polls as well as for comparable and education weights, both calibrated to the US adult public. For comparison, the figure also plots the unweighted percentage of Democrats in the 1952 **American National Election Studies (ANES)** survey, 63%, which is about where it would remain for the next decade.[37] The

[37] If the 1952 ANES is poststratified by *Education*, *Black*, *Female*, and *South*, the estimated Democratic share increases to 64%.

unweighted estimates support Norpoth, Sidman, and Suong's inference that, before 1948, Democratic ID rarely reached the levels recorded in later ANES studies. In fact, in no quarter between 1938 and 1947 did unweighted Democratic ID fall within the 95% confidence interval of the 1952 ANES estimate (59% to 67%), which is indicated by the gray band across the plot.

The picture changes substantially, however, if we weight the polls. Although the weighted and unweighted time series broadly parallel one another – declining through 1946, recovering in 1947–1949, and then dropping again in 1951 – the weighted estimates of Democratic ID are substantially higher than the unweighted ones in almost every quarter.[38] The gap is around 3–5 percentage points for comparable weights and 4–6 points for education weights. According to the weighted analysis, Democrats maintained a clear advantage over Republicans throughout the 1937–1953 period. Moreover, the weighted estimates are statistically distinguishable from the 1952 ANES only for a handful of quarters concentrated in 1946–1948 and 1951–1952. In short, Norpoth, Sidman, and Suong's unweighted analysis appears to have been largely correct about partisan trends but wrong about levels. As a result, the Democrats' victory in 1948 seems less like a realignment and more like a local high point for a party that had been the majority coalition since at least the mid-1930s.

In addition to shedding new light on debates about the timing of the 1930s–1940s partisan realignment, this analysis also provides a nice illustration of the statistical value of using the survey weights. Ameliorating the polls' underrepresentation of Southern, black, female, and lower-class Americans leads to substantially higher estimates of Democratic identification in the mass public. Although the gap between the unweighted and comparable-weights estimates narrowed between 1937 and 1953, suggesting that firms' sampling procedures became more representative over time, the two lines never fully converge. It is also worth noting that the trend-line for the comparable weights is closer to the education trend-line than to the unweighted one. This suggests that the comparable weights are almost (though not quite) as effective as the education weights at mitigating the Republican bias in the raw samples.

## 5.5 Example Code

The Code Ocean capsule for this section is published at `https://doi.org/10.24433/CO.0010101.v1`.

[38] Comparable weights are not available after the third quarter of 1952 because polls after that point did not ask about phone ownership.

Listing 5.1 Setup

```
1  ### Packages
2  library(tidyverse)                    # for useful utilities
3  library(haven)                        # for reading Stata files
4  library(survey)                       # for analyzing complex surveys
5
6  ### Functions
7  load_to_env <- function (RData, env = new.env()) {
8      load(RData, env)
9      return(env)
10 }
11 create_targets <- function (target_design, target_formula) {
12     target_mf <- model.frame(target_formula, model.frame(target_design))
13     target_mm <- model.matrix(target_formula, target_mf)
14     wts <- weights(target_design)
15     colSums(target_mm * wts) / sum(wts)
16 }
17
18 ### Targets
19 target_env <- load_to_env("data/targets.RData")
20 ls(target_env)                        # targets differ by phone question
21
22 ### Poll
23 aipo0380 <- read_dta("data/AIPO0380FW.dta") %>%
24     mutate_if(is.labelled, as_factor)
```

Listing 5.2 Weighting

```
1  ### Phone wording code (some polls have split sample, but not this one)
2  phone_wording <- aipo0380$code_k[1]
3  target_ds <- target_env[[paste0("pop.ds.W", phone_wording)]]
4
5  ### Target populations
6  vap_ds <- subset(target_ds, YEAR == aipo0380$YEAR[1]) # voting-age pop
7  vep_ds <- subset(vap_ds,                              # voting-eligible pop
8                   SOUTH11 == "Non-South" | BLACK == "White")
9
10 ### Formula for auxiliary vector
11 aux_form <- ~PHONE*FEMALE + PHONE*REGION4 + PHONE*PROF + PHONE*BLACK +
12     FEMALE*REGION4 + FEMALE*PROF + FEMALE*BLACK + SOUTH*PROF + SIZE3 +
13     PHONE*URBAN + FEMALE*URBAN + SOUTH*URBAN + EDU4*FEMALE + EDU4*PHONE +
14     EDU4*REGION4 + EDU4*BLACK + EDU4*PROF + EDU4*URBAN + AGE3*PHONE +
15     AGE3*FEMALE + AGE3*SOUTH + AGE3*EDU4
16
17 ## Targets
18 vap_targets <- create_targets(vap_ds, aux_form)
19 vep_targets <- create_targets(vep_ds, aux_form)
20
21 ### Make sure levels match
22 wt_vars <- all.vars(aux_form)
23 for (v in seq_along(wt_vars)) {
24     var <- wt_vars[v]
25     print(var)
26     (target_levels <- levels(target_ds$variables[[var]]))
27     (aipo_levels <- levels(aipo0380[[var]]))
28     stopifnot(identical(sort(aipo_levels), sort(target_levels)))
29     aipo0380[[var]] <- factor(aipo0380[[var]], target_levels)
30 }
31
32 ### Drop cases with missing values on weighting variables
33 aipo0380_vap <- aipo0380 %>%
34     filter_at(vars(wt_vars), all_vars(!is.na(.)))
35 aipo0380_vep <- aipo0380_vap %>%
```

```
36      filter(SOUTH11 == "Non-South" | BLACK == "White") # drops 3 Southern blacks
37
38 ### Create initial survey designs (assumes SRS)
39 aipo0380_vap_srs <- svydesign(~1, data = aipo0380_vap)
40 aipo0380_vep_srs <- svydesign(~1, data = aipo0380_vep)
41
42 ### Rake
43 aipo0380_vap_ewt <- calibrate(design = aipo0380_vap_srs,
44                               formula = aux_form,
45                               population = vap_targets,
46                               calfun = "raking")
47 aipo0380_vep_ewt <- calibrate(design = aipo0380_vep_srs,
48                               formula = aux_form,
49                               population = vep_targets,
50                               calfun = "raking")
```

Listing 5.3 Results

```
1  ### Weights
2  summary(weights(aipo0380_vap_ewt) / mean(weights(aipo0380_vap_ewt)))
3  summary(weights(aipo0380_vep_ewt) / mean(weights(aipo0380_vep_ewt)))
4  ## Dropping Southern blacks from target pop makes weights somewhat less extreme
5
6  ### Car ownership
7  svymean(~CAR_RECODE, aipo0380_vap_srs, na.rm = TRUE)
8  svymean(~CAR_RECODE, aipo0380_vap_ewt, na.rm = TRUE)
9  svymean(~CAR_RECODE, aipo0380_vep_srs, na.rm = TRUE)
10 svymean(~CAR_RECODE, aipo0380_vep_ewt, na.rm = TRUE)
11 ##> Estimated car ownership voters drops by 4-5 points
12
13 ### Presidential vote
14 svymean(~VOTE_RETRO, aipo0380_vap_srs, na.rm = TRUE)
15 svymean(~VOTE_RETRO, aipo0380_vap_ewt, na.rm = TRUE)
16 svymean(~VOTE_RETRO, aipo0380_vep_srs, na.rm = TRUE)
17 svymean(~VOTE_RETRO, aipo0380_vep_ewt, na.rm = TRUE)
18 ##> Estimated proportion of Dewey (Republican) voters drops by 5 points
```

# 6 Extensions and Conclusion

In this final section, we discuss two methodological extensions to our basic framework. The first is weighting-assisted estimation of causal quantities, such as the population average effect of some intervention or "treatment." The second is **multilevel regression and poststratification (MRP)**, which differs from conventional poststratification in that a multilevel model is used to estimate the mean in each poststratification cell. We conclude with general advice on weighting-based survey inference.

## 6.1 Methodological Extensions

### 6.1.1 Weighting for Causal Quantities

The preceding sections focused on population parameters (e.g., $\mu_y$) whose values would be known with certainty if we could enumerate the entire population. In many cases, however, the quantity of interest is a causal rather than descriptive one (for other perspectives, see Lumley 2010, 203–216; Hainmueller, 2012). Causal effects can be conceptualized as the difference between two "potential" outcomes: $Y_i(1)$, the outcome if unit $i$ were exposed to the cause or "treatment" ($a_i = 1$), and $Y_i(0)$, the outcome if $i$ were not exposed ($a_i = 0$) (Splawa-Neyman 1923; Rubin 1974). Because both potential outcomes cannot be observed for a given unit, the unit-level causal effect

$$\tau_i \equiv Y_i(1) - Y_i(0) \tag{6.1}$$

is fundamentally unobservable. Under certain conditions, however, it is possible to draw inferences about averages and other functions of the unit-level effects, such as the **sample average treatment effect (SATE)**:

$$\begin{aligned} \tau_{\mathcal{S}} &\equiv n_{\mathcal{S}}^{-1} \sum_{i \in \mathcal{S}} \tau_i \\ &= n_{\mathcal{S}}^{-1} \sum_{i \in \mathcal{S}} Y_i(1) - n_{\mathcal{S}}^{-1} \sum_{i \in \mathcal{S}} Y_i(0). \end{aligned} \tag{6.2}$$

The key condition enabling such inferences is the causal analog of the **missing at random (MAR)** assumption for nonresponse: *ignorability*, which stipulates that the potential outcomes are, conditional on covariates, independent of treatment assignment.[39] In the case of a simple randomized experiment, an unbiased estimator for the SATE ($\tau_{\mathcal{S}}$) is given by the treated–control difference of means,

$$\hat{\tau}_{\mathcal{S}} = \frac{\sum_{i \in \mathcal{S}} a_i y_i}{\sum_{i \in \mathcal{S}} a_i} - \frac{\sum_{i \in \mathcal{S}} (1 - a_i) y_i}{\sum_{i \in \mathcal{S}} (1 - a_i)}. \tag{6.3}$$

When treatment is not administered with equal probability, the SATE can still be estimated by weighting units by the inverse of their treatment probability, $v_i = 1/\Pr(a_i = 1)$, or an estimate thereof. The inverse probability–weighted (IPW) estimator,

$$\hat{\tau}_{\mathcal{S}}^{\text{IPW}} = \frac{\sum_{i \in \mathcal{S}} a_i v_i y_i}{\sum_{i \in \mathcal{S}} a_i v_i} - \frac{\sum_{i \in \mathcal{S}} (1 - a_i)(1 - v_i) y_i}{\sum_{i \in \mathcal{S}} (1 - a_i)(1 - v_i)}, \tag{6.4}$$

is the causal analog of the Hájek ratio estimator applied separately to each treatment group.[40]

[39] Ignorability also requires that treatment assignment be nondeterministic.

[40] Strictly speaking, (6.4) is the "stabilized IPW estimator" because it uses the realized (weighted) size of the treated group $\sum_{i \in \mathcal{S}} a_i v_i$ rather than the expected size $\mathrm{E}(n_{a=1})$ (Aronow and Miller 2019, 267). As with the Hájek estimation, this substitution confers efficiency gains at the expense of a rapidly diminishing finite-sample bias.

The SATE is a sample quantity that will in general differ from its population counterpart, the **population average treatment effect (PATE)**:

$$\begin{aligned}\tau_{\mathcal{U}} &\equiv N^{-1}\sum_{i\in\mathcal{U}}\tau_i \\ &= N^{-1}\sum_{i\in\mathcal{U}}Y_i(1) - N^{-1}\sum_{i\in\mathcal{U}}Y_i(0) \\ &= \mu_{Y(1)} - \mu_{Y(0)}. \end{aligned} \tag{6.5}$$

To make inferences about the PATE, it is helpful to view the observed $y_i$ as the result of a two-stage sampling process: first, units and their associated pairs of potential outcomes $\{Y_i(1), Y_i(1)\}$ are sampled from the population, and then the treatment assignment mechanism samples one of those potential outcomes to be revealed as $y_i$. If the experimental sample is a **simple random sample (SRS)** from the population and units are assigned to treatment with constant probability, then the observed outcomes in each treatment group are an SRS from the population distribution of potential outcomes. The treated–control difference of means is thus an unbiased estimate of the PATE.

The same design-based logic extends to more complex sampling and assignment mechanisms. Miratrix et al. (2018), for example, consider the case of survey experiments in which subjects sampled from the population with known probabilities $\pi_i = d_i^{-1}$ are randomly assigned to treated and control conditions with probabilities $v_i$ and $1 - v_i$, respectively.[41] As an estimator for the PATE, they suggest

$$\begin{aligned}\hat{\tau}_{\mathcal{U}}^{\mathrm{HH}} &= \frac{\sum_{i\in\mathcal{S}} a_i d_i v_i y_i}{\sum_{i\in\mathcal{S}} a_i d_i v_i} - \frac{\sum_{i\in\mathcal{S}}(1-a_i)d_i(1-v_i)y_i}{\sum_{i\in\mathcal{S}}(1-a_i)d_i(1-v_i)} \\ &= \hat{\mu}_{Y(1)}^{\mathrm{H}} - \hat{\mu}_{Y(0)}^{\mathrm{H}}. \end{aligned} \tag{6.6}$$

Miratrix et al. call (6.6) the "double-Hájek" estimator because it applies the Hájek ratio estimator separately to the treated and control groups. Like $\hat{\tau}_{\mathcal{S}}^{\mathrm{IPW}}$, $\hat{\tau}_{\mathcal{U}}^{\mathrm{HH}}$ weights by $v_i$ to estimate the SATE, but unlike $\hat{\tau}_{\mathcal{S}}^{\mathrm{IPW}}$ it extrapolates this estimate to the population by weighting by $d_i$ as well.

Even if the experimental sample or respondent set is not a random sample from the population of interest, we may still be able to obtain reasonable estimates of the PATE by weighting the sample. That is, we can replace the design weights $d_i$ in (6.6) with adjustment weights $\tilde{w}_i$. As with descriptive quantities, weights for causal quantities can be calculated via poststratification, raking,

[41] Miratrix et al. (2018) assume $\Pr(a_i = 1)$ is constant and therefore drop $v_i$ from the expression in (6.6).

or other forms of calibration.[42] Moreover, sample effect estimates may be weighted to targets other than the PATE, such as population average treatment effect *among those exposed to treatment*: $\sum_{i \in \mathcal{U}} (\tau_i \mid a_i = 1) / \sum_{i \in \mathcal{U}} a_i$ (e.g., Hartman et al. 2015). Regardless of the target quantity, the assumptions necessary for such causal extrapolation are the same as for descriptive inference. The auxiliary vector used to calibrate the sample must be contain powerful predictors of units' probability of being included in the sample and/or the difference in their potential outcomes, thereby rendering inclusion probabilities and treatment effects approximately independent.

### 6.1.2 Multilevel Regression and Poststratification

Throughout this text, we have confined ourselves to design-based estimators that, given assumptions about the sampling and nonresponse mechanisms, are at least approximately unbiased and whose variances can be estimated from the sampling design alone. These estimators have also been nonparametric in the sense that they do not rely on a parametric model for the outcome $y$. For some problems and purposes, however, a fully model-based approach may be preferable to a design-based one (see, e.g., Little 1993). The advantages of model-based approaches is well illustrated by the increasingly popular technique of MRP (Gelman and Little 1997; Park, Gelman, and Bafumi 2004).

MRP is a three-step process, the workflow of which is summarized in Figure 6.1. The first step is to fit a multilevel model for the outcome variable $y$, typically using a mix of demographic and geographic variables as

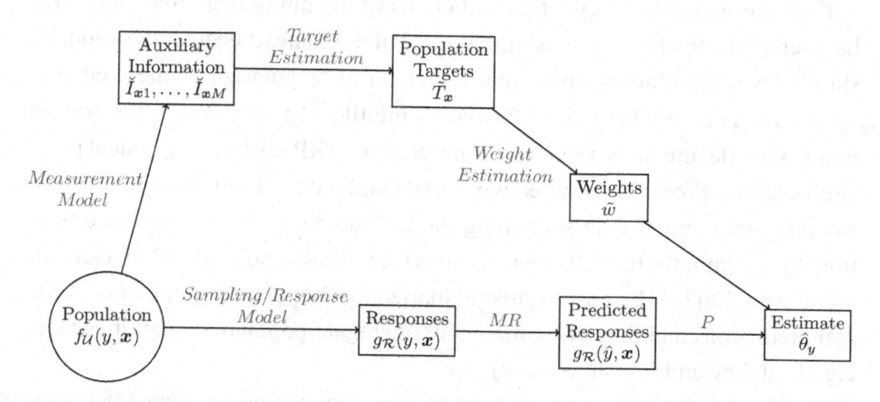


**Figure 6.1** The workflow of multilevel regression and poststratification (MRP).

[42] Alternatively, population units' probabilities of participating in the experiment could be estimated directly via a parametric model, and the estimated probabilities used in an IPW estimator (Stuart et al. 2011).

predictors. At least some of the coefficients in the multilevel model are "random effects," meaning that the coefficients themselves are modeled with a prior distribution, which "shrinks" the coefficient estimates towards the mean of the prior. The second step is to use the model to predict the expected value of $y$ for an exhaustive and mutually exclusive set of subpopulations (cells). The cell predictions are thus a compromise between the data in the cell itself and information derived from the rest of the population. In the third step, poststratification, the cell predictions are weighted by their population proportions to produce estimates for larger subpopulations or the population as a whole. Thus, for example, one might generate estimates for the US population by taking a weighted average of the estimates for cells defined by race and state.

The MRP estimator can be viewed as a modification of the conventional poststratification estimator given in (2.2), with the observed response $y_i$ of unit $i$ in cell $c$ replaced with its predicted response $\hat{y}_{c[i]}$:

$$\hat{\mu}_y^{\text{MRP}} = \frac{\sum_{i \in \mathcal{R}} \tilde{w}_{c[i]}^{\text{PS}} \hat{y}_{c[i]}}{\sum_{i \in \mathcal{R}} \tilde{w}_{c[i]}^{\text{PS}}}, \tag{6.7}$$

where $\tilde{w}_{c[i]}^{\text{PS}} = (\tilde{P}_{c[i]}/\hat{P}_{c[i]}^{\text{H}}) \times d_i$ is the poststratification weight for unit $i$ in cell $c$. In practice, because $\hat{y}_{c[i]}$ is constant within cells, the estimator in (6.7) can be simplified to $\hat{\mu}_y^{\text{MRP}} = \sum_{c \in \mathcal{U}} \tilde{P}_c \hat{y}_c / \sum_{c \in \mathcal{U}} \tilde{P}_c$, the population-weighted average of the cell predictions. The advantage of the latter estimator, and of MRP generally, is that it can be implemented even if there are empty cells, since their values are imputed.

Even for non-empty cells, the predictions of the multilevel model may still be preferable to the raw (design-based) cell estimates because the model's shrinkage of the random effects has the effect of "regularizing" the predicted values $\hat{y}_c$. This regularization, for which multilevel regression is but one of many potential methods, reduces the variance of MRP relative to classical poststratification. From this perspective, MRP can be thought of as an alternative to raking that, rather than smoothing the cell targets as raking does (see Section 2.1.2), smooths the cell means instead (see. Elliott and Little 2000; Gelman and Carlin 2002). The cost of this regularization is typically some bias in the cell predictions and thus in estimators of aggregate population quantities (see, e.g., Caughey and Warshaw 2019).

Despite this bias, there are at least two conditions under which MRP may be preferable to classical design-based poststratification. The first condition is if the partition of the population required for unbiased estimation – that is, the set of cells within which either $\rho$ or $y$ is homogeneous – defines cells that are empty in the sample, making classical poststratification impossible. In this case, MRP's model-based imputation of the empty cells may result in less bias than poststratification with coarser auxiliary vector (e.g., one with collapsed cells). The second condition is if poststratification, while feasible, yields estimators with unacceptably high variance. If this is so, even if the bias of MRP is larger than design-based poststratification, it may nevertheless have lower **mean squared error (MSE)**. In sum, MRP can sometimes have smaller bias than design-based alternatives, and even when its bias is larger, MRP is often more efficient. These conditions are especially common in the context of estimation for small subpopulations, such as states (Lax and Phillips 2009) or congressional districts (Warshaw and Rodden 2012), for which sample sizes are often too small for reliable design-based inference.

## 6.2 Concluding Advice

This Element has elaborated a general approach to addressing sampling and nonresponse bias in surveys. Although it has described a number of specific methods and procedures, in our view these details are less important than the general workflow that we advocate. This workflow consists of two basic tasks: target estimation and weight estimation. Despite the conventional emphasis on the latter, both are important, and reliance on unrealistic assumptions (whether explicit or implicit) in either task can result in poor estimates. It is therefore essential that survey analysts give careful thought to their models of the sampling process, nonresponse mechanism, and measurement of auxiliary information, drawing on substantive knowledge as well as statistical criteria. That said, it is rare that the survey analyst fully understands the measurement and sampling/nonresponse processes. As a consequence, it is unrealistic to expect post hoc adjustment, however skillful, to eliminate bias completely. Even as auxiliary information become increasingly abundant, there is no substitute for the laborious work of designing and implementing high-quality surveys in which the problems weighting is supposed to fix are as minimal as possible.

## 6.3 Example Code

The Code Ocean capsule for this section is published at `https://doi.org/10.24433/CO.5307324.v1`.

Listing 6.1 Setup

```
1  ### Packages
2  library(tidyverse)                         # for useful utilities
3  library(survey)                            # for analyzing complex surveys
4
5  ### Functions
6  create_targets <- function (target_design, target_formula) {
7      target_mf <- model.frame(target_formula, model.frame(target_design))
```

```
8      target_mm <- model.matrix(target_formula, target_mf)
9      wts <- weights(target_design)
10     colSums(target_mm * wts) / sum(wts)
11 }
12 load_to_env <- function (RData, env = new.env()) {
13     load(RData, env)
14     return(env)
15 }
```

Listing 6.2 Weighting for causal inference

```
1  ## Data (from replication files for Miratrix et al. 2018, "Worth Weighting?")
2
3  experiments <- read.csv("data/Survey_Experiment_Data_table.csv")
4
5  ucb <- experiments %>%
6      filter(Survery == "UCB_Follow" & Outcome == "typicalzero") %>%
7      droplevels()
8
9  ucb_awt <- svydesign(~1, weights = ~weight, data = ucb) # YouGov weights
10 ucb_srs <- svydesign(~1, weights = ~1, data = ucb)      # unweighted
11
12 ## Estimate effects in survey experiment
13 ### Mean by treatment group (= mean of potential outcomes, if tr probs same)
14 svyby(~Y, ~T, ucb_awt, svymean, na.rm = TRUE)
15 ### Difference of means (double-Hajek esimator)
16 svycontrast(svyby(~Y, ~T, ucb_awt, svymean, na.rm = TRUE),
17             quote(`Democratic report` - `Republican report`))
18 ### Same as regression coefficient in:
19 summary(svyglm(Y ~ T, ucb_awt))
20 ### Compare with unweighted (small difference)
21 summary(svyglm(Y ~ T, ucb_srs))
22
23 ## Calibrating to PID
24
25 ### PID is a strong predictor of Y and of the treatment effect:
26 summary(svyglm(Y ~ T * pid, ucb_awt))
27 ### Thus, calibrating to PID may increase the precision of the estimates.
28
29 ### This same procedure could also be used to adjust for unequal treatment
30 ### assignment probabilities (i.e., if this were an observational study rather
31 ### than an experiment).
32
33 ### Recode treatment to {-1/2, 1/2} so that its target is 0
34 ucb_awt <- update(ucb_awt, T2 = as.integer(T) - 3/2)
35
36 ### PID targets (from other experiments)
37 other_experiments <- experiments %>%
38     filter(!is.na(pid) & pid != "Other " & Survery != "UCB_Follow") %>%
39     droplevels()
40 other_awt <- svydesign(~1, weights = ~1, data = other_experiments)
41 pid_targets <- c(create_targets(other_awt, ~pid),
42                  T2 = 0, `pidIndependent:T2` = 0, `pidRepublican:T2` = 0)
43
44 ### Calibrate
45 ucb_awt_pid <- calibrate(subset(ucb_awt, !is.na(pid)), ~pid * T2, pid_targets)
46
47 ### Results
48 svyby(~pid, ~T, ucb_awt, svymean, na.rm = TRUE, keep.var = TRUE)
49 svyby(~pid, ~T, ucb_awt_pid, svymean, na.rm = TRUE, keep.var = TRUE) # balanced
50
51 summary(svyglm(Y ~ T, subset(ucb_awt, !is.na(pid))))
52 summary(svyglm(Y ~ T, ucb_awt_pid))     # slightly more precise
```

Listing 6.3 Multilevel regression and poststratification

```
1  ### Packages
2  library(arm)
3  library(haven)                          # for reading Stata files
4
5  ### Poll
6  aipo0380 <- read_dta("data/AIPO0380FW.dta") %>%
7      mutate_if(is.labelled, as_factor) %>%
8      mutate(dem_retro = case_when(
9                  VOTE_RETRO == "FDR" ~ 1,
10                 VOTE_RETRO == "Dewey" ~ 0,
11                 TRUE ~ NA_real_))
12 poll_year <- aipo0380$YEAR[1]
13
14 ### Targets
15 target_env <- load_to_env("data/targets.RData")
16
17 ### Phone wording code (some polls have split sample, but not this one)
18 phone_wording <- aipo0380$code_k[1]
19 target_ds <- target_env[[paste0("pop.ds.W", phone_wording)]]
20
21 ### Target population
22 vap_ds <- subset(target_ds, YEAR == poll_year) # voting-age pop
23
24 ### Make sure levels match
25 aipo0380 <- aipo0380 %>%
26     mutate(StPOAbrv = factor(StPOAbrv, levels(vap_ds$variables$StPOAbrv)))
27
28 ### Survey design
29 aipo0380_srs <- svydesign(~1, weights = ~1, data = aipo0380)
30
31 ### Cell distribution in population (%)
32 round(svytable(~BLACK + StPOAbrv, vap_ds, round = FALSE, Ntotal = 100), 2)
33
34 ### Cell distribution in sample (many empty)
35 round(svytable(~BLACK + StPOAbrv, aipo0380_srs))
36
37 ### (1) Model outcome (presidential vote) -- [Note: not very sophisticated]
38 pres_mod <- glmer(dem_retro ~ BLACK + (1 | StPOAbrv),
39                   data = aipo0380,
40                   family = binomial)
41 display(pres_mod)
42
43 ### (2) Predict cell means
44 pred_input <- svytable(~BLACK + StPOAbrv, vap_ds) %>%
45     as.data.frame() %>%
46     filter(StPOAbrv != "SC")           # missing in poll so no intercept est.
47 pred_output <- predict(pres_mod, pred_input, type = "response")
48 pred_df <- data.frame(pred_input, Yhat = pred_output)
49 head(pred_df)
50
51 ### (3) Poststratify
52 pred_ds <- svydesign(~1, weights = ~Freq, data = pred_df)
53
54 svyby(~dem_retro, ~StPOAbrv, aipo0380_srs, FUN = svymean,
55       keep.var = FALSE, na.rm = TRUE)
56
57 #### Compare with raw estimates
58 comp_df <- data.frame(
59     StPOAbrv = svyby(~dem_retro, ~StPOAbrv, aipo0380_srs, FUN = svymean,
60                      keep.var = FALSE, na.rm = TRUE)$StPOAbrv,
61     Raw = svyby(~dem_retro, ~StPOAbrv, aipo0380_srs, FUN = svymean,
62                 keep.var = FALSE, na.rm = TRUE)$statistic,
63     MRP = svyby(~Yhat, ~StPOAbrv, pred_ds, FUN = svymean,
```

```
64                      keep.var = FALSE, na.rm = TRUE)$statistic)
65
66  comp_df %>% mutate(Diff = MRP - Raw) %>% arrange(abs(Diff))
67
68  comp_df %>%
69      ggplot(aes(x = Raw, y = MRP, label = StPOAbrv)) +
70      xlim(0, 1) +
71      ylim(0, 1) +
72      geom_text() +
73      geom_abline(intercept = 0, slope = 1)
```

# Glossary

**ACS** *American Community Survey*. 41

**adjustment weight** ($\tilde{w}_i$) A weight assigned to each responding unit $i$ after the sample has been realized, typically as a means of adjusting for bias due to nonrandom sampling and/or nonresponse but also potentially for increasing estimators' precision. 8, 75

**adjustment weighting** The ex post assignment of weights to sampled units, typically as a means of increasing the representativeness of samples and thereby decreasing the bias and/or variance of estimators of population quantities. Contrast with inverse-probability weighting, which derives weights from (ex ante) features of the sampling design. Specific types of adjustment weighting include poststratification, raking, and calibration. 8

**AIPO** *American Institute of Public Opinion*. 49

**ANES** *American National Election Studies*. 3, 63

**AT&T** *American Telephone and Telegraph*. 25

**auxiliary vector** ($\boldsymbol{z}_i$) A vector defined for each member $i$ of the **respondent set** $\mathcal{R}$, each element of which is a function of one or more **auxiliary variables**. Calibrating a sample to a population with respect to an auxiliary vector $\boldsymbol{z}_i$ entails finding **adjustment weights** $\tilde{\boldsymbol{w}}$ that satisfy the constraints $\tilde{T}_{\boldsymbol{x}k} = \sum_{i \in \mathcal{R}} \tilde{w}_i z_{ik}$, $k \in 1 \ldots K$, where $\tilde{T}_{\boldsymbol{x}}$ is a vector of $K$ **population targets**. 17

**auxiliary information** ($\breve{I}_{\boldsymbol{x}}$) Data on the joint and/or marginal distributions of one or more **auxiliary variables** in the target population. 4, 77

**auxiliary variable** ($x$) A variable measured in the sample, data on whose population distribution are available from auxiliary information. *see* auxiliary information, 8, 75, 77, 78

**bootstrap** A family of methods that involve taking repeated samples from an empirical distribution $\hat{F}$, itself a sample from an unknown distribution $F$, as a means of estimating the sampling distributions of functions (i.e., parameters) of $F$. 7, 15

**calibration** A method of adjustment weighting in which a sample is "calibrated" to the target population by finding adjustment weights that satisfy a set of **population targets** while deviating as little as possible from a set of base weights (e.g., design weights). *see* adjustment weighting, 8, 17, 79

**CCES** *Cooperative Congressional Election Study*. 41

**CPS** *Current Population Study*. 10

**DAE** *difference in absolute error*. 61

**design effect due to weighting** ($\text{deff}_{\text{Kish}}$) An estimate of the ratio of the variance of a weighted estimator to the ratio of an unweighted one, proposed by Kish (1965) as an indicator of the degree to which unequal weights make estimators less precise. 20, 42

**design weight** ($d_i$) A weight assigned to each sampled unit $i$ based on the sampling design, typically equal to the inverse of the unit's ex ante probability of being selected. 6

**Dirichlet** A multivariate distribution used to model data that range between 0 and 1 and whose values sum to 1 (e.g., proportions). It is denoted $\text{Dir}(\alpha)$, where the parameter vector $\alpha$ has the same length as the number of proportions being modeled. The Dirichlet is the multivariate generalization of the beta distribution and is closely related to the Multinomial distribution for categorical counts. *see* Multinomial, 30

**EI** *ecological inference*: Using aggregate data (e.g., on the proportion of the population that is African American and on the proportion with a telephone) to draw inferences about the properties of individual units (e.g., the proportion of African Americans who own a telephone). 28, 54

**entropy weighting** A species of calibration that employs the entropy distance $D^{\text{ent}}(\tilde{w}_i, d_i) = w_i \log(w_i/d_i)$. *see* raking, 17, 43, 78

**GREG** *generalized regression (estimator)*. 31

**Hájek estimator** A variant of the Horvitz-Thompson estimator of the mean that substitutes the realized weighted sample size for the expected one; also known as the ratio estimator of the mean. 6

**HT** *Horvitz-Thompson*. 5

**IID** *independent and identically distributed*. 8

**IPUMS** *Integrated Public Use Microdata Series*. 25, 51

**item nonresponse** The presence of missing values on some but not all survey items. *cf.* unit nonresponse, 5

**joint distribution** The density or probability of combinations of values of two or more variables. *cf.* marginal distribution, 5, 13

**linear weighting** A species of calibration that employs the chi-square distance $D^{\chi^2}(\tilde{w}_i, d_i) = (\tilde{w}_i - d_i)^2/d_i$. *see* poststratification, 17, 31, 41, 78

**MAR** *missing at random*: Data are MAR if, given the observed values and missingness pattern, elements' probability of being missing does not depend on the values of the missing elements. *see* MCAR, 8, 67

**marginal distribution** The unconditional density or probability of each value a given variable, irrespective of the values of other variables. *cf.* joint distribution, 15

**MCAR** *missing completely at random*: Data are MCAR if the probability of missingness does not depend on either the observed or the unobserved values of the data (i.e., is independent of both). *see* MAR

**measurement model** A characterization of the process linking the true population distribution of the **auxiliary variables** to **auxiliary information** on those variables. 24

**MOC** *method of composition*: A simulation-based method of estimating the marginal distribution $h(y)$ given the conditional distribution $f(y|\boldsymbol{x})$. In the bivariate case, this involves repeating two steps: (1) draw $x^* \sim g(x)$; (2) draw $y^* \sim f(y|x^*)$. The resulting collection of $y^*$ draws will be an IID sample from $h(y)$. 32

**MRP** *multilevel regression and poststratification*: A method of opinion measurement, especially for small-area estimation, in which opinion in disjoint subpopulations is modeled hierarchically as a function of geographic and/or demographic characteristics. Opinion in larger (sub)populations is then estimated as a weighted (i.e., poststratified) average of the model-based subpopulation estimates. 66

**MSE** *mean squared error*: A measure of the inaccuracy of an estimator, defined as the average (across repeated samples) of the squared differences between the true and estimated values of a parameter; or, equivalently, the variance plus the squared bias. 15, 71

**Multinomial** A generalization of the binomial distribution used to model the number of successes across several categories given a fixed number of independent trials. 29

**nonresponse bias** Bias due to systematic differences in sampled units' probabilities of providing valid responses. *see* unit nonresponse, 3

**NORC** *National Opinion Research Council*. 49

**observation model** The component of a state-space model that relates the latent state to its observed indicators. *see* transition model, 28

**OPOR** *Office of Public Opinion Research.* 49

**PATE** ($\tau_{\mathcal{U}}$) *population average treatment effect*: The average causal effect of treatment across units in the population. 68

**population target** ($\tilde{T}_{\boldsymbol{x}}$) An estimate of the population mean or total of a function of one or more **auxiliary variables** $\boldsymbol{x}$, to which a sample can be "calibrated" by finding weights such that the analogous moments in the weighted sample match the targets. 8, 75, 76, 79

**poststratification** A type of **linear weighting** in which units are categorized into a set of exhaustive and mutually exclusive strata (cells) assigned weights such that the cells' sample proportions match a set of target proportions. 8, 14

**probability sampling** A process of selecting survey subjects or other units in which the probability of each possible sample from the population (and thus the sampling probability of each unit) is known ex ante. *cf.* quota sampling, 3, 49

**quota sampling** A sampling method in which units are selected according to predetermined proportions (quotas) of each demographic type, but within these quotas units are sampled purposively rather than according to ex ante probabilities. *cf.* probability sampling, 2, 39, 50

**raking** A type of **entropy weighting** in which iterative proportional fitting is used to find weights that ensure that the sample matches a set of marginal population totals. 8, 15

**RDD** *random digit dialing*: A method of selecting respondents for a telephone survey based on the random generation of telephone numbers. 3, 39

**respondent set** The set of sampled subjects who provide valid responses to all relevant survey variables. 5, 75

**response probability** ($\rho_i$) The probability that unit $i$, if sampled, will provide valid answers to the survey. 7

**response influence** ($\omega_i$) The inverse response probability of unit $i$. *see* response probability, 16

**sampling probability** ($\pi_i$) The ex ante probability that population unit $i$ will be selected for inclusion in the sample. 5

**sampling bias** Bias due to systematic discrepancies between the target population and the set of units selected for inclusion in the sample. *see* nonresponse bias, 3

**SATE** ($\tau_S$) *sample average treatment effect*: The average causal effect of treatment across units in a given sample. 67

**SRC** *Survey Research Center*. 3, 59

**SRS** *simple random sample*: A sample in which the inclusion probability for each population unit is known, independent, and equal. 5, 14, 40, 68

**SSF** *synthetic sampling frame*. 27

**target estimation** The process of calculating **population targets** for use in **calibration** or other forms of weighting. 13, 24

**transition model** The component of a state-space model that describes how the latent state evolves over time. *see* observation model, 29

**unit nonresponse** The failure of one or more sampled units to provide valid responses to any of the survey items. *cf.* item nonresponse, 5

**VAP** *voting-age population*. 53

**VEP** *voting-eligible population*. 53

**weight estimation** The creation, typically after a survey has been completed, of adjustment weights intended to reduce the bias or variance of survey estimates. 13

# References

Andridge, Rebecca R., and Roderick J. A. Little. 2011. "Proxy Pattern-Mixture Analysis for Survey Nonresponse." *Journal of Official Statistics* 27 (2): 153–180.

Ansolabehere, Stephen, and Eitan Hersh. 2012. "Validation: What Big Data Reveal About Survey Misreporting and the Real Electorate." *Political Analysis* 20 (4): 437–459.

Ansolabehere, Stephen, and Douglas Rivers. 2013. "Cooperative Survey Research." *Annual Review of Political Science* 16: 307–329.

Aronow, Peter M., and Benjamin T. Miller. 2019. *Foundations of Agnostic Statistics*. New York: Cambridge University Press.

Baum, Matthew A., and Samuel Kernell. 2001. "Economic Class and Popular Support for Franklin Roosevelt in War and Peace." *Public Opinion Quarterly* 65 (2): 198–229.

Berinsky, Adam J. 2006. "American Public Opinion in the 1930s and 1940s: The Analysis of Quota-Controlled Sample Survey Data." *Public Opinion Quarterly* 70 (4): 499–529.

Berinsky, Adam J., Eleanor Neff Powell, Eric Schickler, and Ian Brett Yohai. 2011. "Revisiting Public Opinion in the 1930s and 1940s." *PS: Political Science & Politics* 44 (3): 515–520.

Berinsky, Adam J., and Eric Schickler. 2011. *The American Mass Public in the 1930s and 1940s [Computer file]*. Individual surveys conducted by the Gallup Organization [producers], 1936–1945: Roper Center for Public Opinion Research, University of Connecticut [distributor].

Bethlehem, Jelke G. 1988. "Reduction of Nonresponse Bias Through Regression Estimation." *Journal of Official Statistics* 4 (3): 251–260.

Bethlehem, Jelke, Fannie Cobben, and Barry Schouten. 2011. *Handbook of Nonresponse in Household Surveys*. Hoboken, NJ: Wiley.

Binder, D. A., and A. Théberge. 1988. "Estimating the Variance of Raking-Ratio Estimators." *Canadian Journal of Statistics* 16: 47–55.

Brick, J. Michael, and Jill M. Montaquila. 2009. "Nonresponse and Weighting." In *Sample Surveys: Design, Methods and Applications*, edited by Danny Pfeffermann and C. R. Rao, vol. 29A, 163–185. Handbook of Statistics. Elsevier.

British Polling Council. 2016. "Performance of the Polls in the EU Referendum." June 24. Accessed October 26, 2019. www.britishpollingcouncil.org/performance-of-the-polls-in-the-eu-referendum/.

Bunche, Ralph J. 1973. *The Political Status of the Negro in the Age of FDR*. Edited by Dewey W. Grantham. Chicago: University of Chicago Press.

Caldeira, Gregory A. 1987. "Public Opinion and the U.S. Supreme Court: FDR's Court-Packing Plan." *American Political Science Review* 81 (4): 1139–1153.

Caughey, Devin, and Erin Hartman. 2017. "Target Selection as Variable Selection: Using the Lasso to Select Auxiliary Vectors for the Construction of Survey Weights." Paper presented at the Annual Meeting of the Society for Political Methodology, University of Wisconsin–Madison, Madison, WI, July 13. `https://ssrn.com/abstract=3494436`.

Caughey, Devin, and Mallory Wang. 2014. "Bayesian Population Interpolation and Lasso-Based Target Selection in Survey Weighting." Paper presented at the Annual Meeting of the Society for Political Methodology, University of Georgia, Athens, GA, July 24. `https://ssrn.com/abstract=3494430`.

2019. "Dynamic Ecological Inference for Time-Varying Population Distributions Based on Sparse, Irregular, and Noisy Marginal Data." *Political Analysis*. 27 (3): 388–396. `https://doi.0rg/10.1017/pan.2019.4`.

Caughey, Devin, and Christopher Warshaw. 2019. "Public Opinion in Subnational Politics." *Journal of Politics* 81 (Symposium on Subnational Policymaking): 352–363.

Cochran, William G. 1977. *Sampling Techniques*. 3rd ed. New York: Wiley.

Converse, Jean M. 1987. *Survey Research in the United States: Roots and Emergence*. Berkeley: University of California Press.

Davison, A. C., and David V. Hinkley. 1997. *Bootstrap Methods and Their Application*. New York: Cambridge University Press.

Deming, W. Edwards, and F. Frederick Stephan. 1940. "On a Least Squares Adjustment of a Sampled Frequency Table When the Expected Marginal Totals Are Known." *Annals of Mathematical Statistics* 11 (4): 427–444.

Dever, Jill A., and Richard Valliant. 2010. "A Comparison of Variance Estimators for Poststratification to Estimated Control Totals." *Survey Methodology* 36 (1): 45–56.

2016. "General Regression Estimation Adjusted for Undercoverage and Estimated Control Totals." *Journal of Survey Statistics and Methodology* 4 (3): 289–318.

Deville, Jean-Claude. 1991. "A Theory of Quota Surveys." *Survey Methodology* 17 (2): 163–181.

2000. "Simultaneous Calibration of Several Surveys." In *Combining Data from Different Sources*, Proceedings of Statistics Canada Symposium 99, 207–212. Ottawa: Statistics Canada.

Deville, Jean-Claude, and Carl-Erik Särndal. 1992. “Calibration Estimators in Survey Sampling.” *Journal of the American Statistical Association* 87 (418): 376–382.

Dixon, John, and Clyde Tucker. 2010. “Survey Nonresponse.” In *Handbook of Survey Research*, 2nd ed., edited by Peter V. Marsden and James D. Wright, 593–630. Bingley, UK: Emerald.

Economic Behavior Program, Survey Research Center, University of Michigan. 1948. *Survey of Consumer Finances*. Ann Arbor, MI: Institute for Social Research, Social Science Archive [producer], 1973. Ann Arbor, MI: Inter-university Consortium for Political and Social Research [distributor], 2002. `http://doi.org/10.3886/ICPSR03601.v1`.

Elliott, Michael R., and Roderick J. A. Little. 2000. “Model-Based Alternatives to Trimming Survey Weights.” *Journal of Official Statistics* 16 (3): 191–209.

Enns, Peter K., and Julianna Koch. 2013. “Public Opinion in the U.S. States: 1956 to 2010.” *State Politics & Policy Quarterly* 13 (3): 349–372.

Field, Alexander J. 2006. “Table Dg34-45: Telephone industry – telephones, access lines, wire, employees, and plant: 1876–2000.” In *Historical Statistics of the United States, Earliest Times to the Present: Millennial Edition*, edited by Susan B. Carter, Scott Sigmund Gartner, Michael R. Haines, Alan L. Olmstead, Richard Sutch, and Gavin Wright. New York: Cambridge University Press. `http://hsus.cambridge.org/SeriesDg8-116`.

Folger, John K., and Charles B. Nam. 1964. “Educational Trends from Census Data.” *Demography* 1 (1): 247–257.

Freedman, David A. 2001. “Ecological Inference and the Ecological Fallacy.” In *International Encyclopaedia of the Social and Behavioural Sciences*, edited by N. J. Smelser and P. B. Baltes, 6:4027–4030. New York: Elsevier.

Gelman, Andrew. 2007. “Struggles with Survey Weighting and Regression Modeling.” *Statistical Science* 22 (2): 153–164.

Gelman, Andrew, and John B. Carlin. 2002. “Poststratification and Weighting Adjustments.” In *Survey Nonresponse*, edited by Robert M. Graves, Don A. Dillman, John L. Eltinge, and Roderick J. A. Little, 289–302. New York: Wiley.

Gelman, Andrew, and Thomas C. Little. 1997. “Poststratification into Many Categories Using Hierarchical Logistic Regression.” *Survey Methodology* 23 (2): 127–135.

Groves, Robert M. 2006. “Nonresponse Rates and Nonresponse Bias in Household Surveys.” *Public Opinion Quarterly* 70 (5): 646–675.

Guandalini, Alessio, and Yves Tillé. 2017. "Design-Based Estimators Calibrated on Estimated Totals from Multiple Surveys." *International Statistical Review* 85 (2): 250–269.

Hainmueller, Jens. 2012. "Entropy Balancing for Causal Effects: A Multivariate Reweighting Method to Produce Balanced Samples in Observational Studies." *Political Analysis* 20 (1): 25–46.

Hájek, Jaroslav. 1958. "On the Theory of Ratio Estimates." *Applied Mathematics* 3 (5): 384–398.

Hartman, Erin, Richard Grieve, Roland Ramsahai, and Jasjeet S. Sekhon. 2015. "From Sample Average Treatment Effect to Population Average Treatment Effect on the Treated: Combining Experimental with Observational Studies to Estimate Population Treatment Effects." *Journal of the Royal Statistical Society: Series A (Statistics in Society)* 178 (3): 757–778.

Hillygus, Sunshine. 2016. "The Practice of Survey Research: Changes and Challenges." In *New Directions in Public Opinion*, 2nd ed., edited by Adam J. Berinsky, 34–53. New York: Routledge.

Horvitz, D. G., and D. J. Thompson. 1952. "A Generalization of Sampling without Replacement from a Finite Universe." *Journal of the American Statistical Association* 47: 663–685.

Hur, Aram, and Christopher H. Achen. 2013. "Coding Voter Turnout Responses in the Current Population Survey." *Public Opinion Quarterly* 77 (4): 985–993.

Ireland, C. T., and S. Kullback. 1968. "Contingency Tables with Given Marginals." *Biometrika* 55 (1): 179–188.

Kalton, Graham, and Ismael Flores-Cervantes. 2003. "Weighting Methods." *Journal of Official Statistics* 19 (2): 81–97.

Kastellec, Jonathan P., Jeffrey R. Lax, Michael Malecki, and Justin H. Phillips. 2015. "Polarizing the Electoral Connection: Partisan Representation in Supreme Court Confirmation Politics." *Journal of Politics* 77 (3): 787–804.

Kennedy, Courtney, Mark Blumenthal, Scott Clement et al. 2018. "An Evaluation of the 2016 Election Polls in the United States." *Public Opinion Quarterly* 82 (1): 1–33.

Key, V. O., Jr. 1949. *Southern Politics in State and Nation*. New York: Knopf.

King, Gary, Ori Rosen, and Martin A. Tanner. 2004. "Information in Ecological Inference: An Introduction." In *Ecological Inference: New Methodological Strategies*, edited by Gary King, Ori Rosen, and Martin A. Tanner, 1–12. New York: Cambridge University Press.

Kish, Leslie. 1965. *Survey Sampling*. New York: Wiley.

Kott, Phillip S. 2006. "Using Calibration Weighting to Adjust for Nonresponse and Coverage Errors." *Survey Methodology* 32 (2): 133–142.

Lax, Jeffrey R., and Justin H. Phillips. 2009. "How Should We Estimate Public Opinion in The States?" *American Journal of Political Science* 53 (1): 107–121.

Leeman, Lucas, and Fabio Wasserfallen. 2017. "Extending the Use and Prediction Precision of Subnational Public Opinion Estimation." *American Journal of Political Science* 61 (4): 1003–1022.

Leeuw, E. de, and W. de Heer. 2002. "Trends in Household Survey Nonresponse: A Longitudinal and International Comparison." In *Survey Nonresponse*, edited by R. M. Groves, D. A. Dillman, J. L. Eltinge, and R. J. A. Little, 41–54. New York: Wiley.

Little, R. J. A. 1993. "Post-Stratification: A Modeler's Perspective." *Journal of the American Statistical Association* 88 (423): 1001–1012.

Little, Roderick J. A., and Mei-Miau Wu. 1991. "Models for Contingency Tables With Known Margins When Target and Sampled Populations Differ." *Journal of the American Statistical Association* 86 (413): 87–95.

Little, Roderick J., and Sonya Vartivarian. 2005. "Does Weighting for Nonresponse Increase the Variance of Survey Means?" *Survey Methodology* 31 (2): 161–168.

Luevano, Patricia. 1994. *Response Rates in the National Election Studies, 1948–1992*. Technical report 44. March. `www.electionstudies.org/Library/papers/documents/nes010162.pdf`.

Lumley, Thomas S. 2010. *Complex Surveys: A Guide to Analysis Using R*. Hoboken, NJ: Wiley.

Mackuen, Michael B., Robert S. Erikson, and James A. Stimson. 1989. "Macropartisanship." *American Political Science Review* 83 (4): 1125–1142.

Marken, Stephanie. 2018. "Still Listening: The State of Telephone Surveys." Gallup, *Methodology Blog*, January 18. `http://news.gallup.com/opinion/methodology/225143/listening-state-telephone-surveys.aspx`.

McDonald, Michael. 2019. "CPS Vote Over-Report and Non-Response Bias Correction." Accessed October 2. `http://www.electproject.org/home/voter-turnout/cps-methodology`.

Mickey, Robert W. 2015. *Paths Out of Dixie: The Democratization of Authoritarian Enclaves in America's Deep South*. Princeton, NJ: Princeton University Press.

Miratrix, Luke, Jasjeet S. Sekhon, Alexander G. Theodoridis, and Luis F. Campos. 2018. "Worth Weighting? How to Think About and Use Weights in Survey Experiments." *Political Analysis* 26:275–291.

Mosteller, Frederick, Herbert Hyman, Philip J. McCarthy, Eli S. Marks, and David B. Truman, eds. 1949. *The Pre-Election Polls of 1948*. New York: Social Science Research Council.

Moy, Corrine. 2015. "Fit-for-purpose sampling." *International Journal of Market Research* 57 (3): 491–494.

Norpoth, Helmut, Andrew H. Sidman, and Clara H. Suong. 2013. "Polls and Elections: The New Deal Realignment in Real Time." *Presidential Studies Quarterly* 43 (1): 146–166.

Park, David K., Andrew Gelman, and Joseph Bafumi. 2004. "Bayesian Multilevel Estimation with Poststratification: State-Level Estimates from National Polls." *Political Analysis* 12 (4): 375–385.

Pew Research Center. 2016. *As Election Nears, Voters Divided Over Democracy and "Respect"*. Technical report. October. `www.people-press.org/2016/10/27/as-election-nears-voters-divided-over-democracy-and-respect/`.

Peytchev, Andy. 2012. "Multiple Imputation for Unit Nonresponse and Measurement Error." *Public Opinion Quarterly* 76 (2): 214–237.

Quinn, Kevin M. 2004. "Ecological Inference in the Presence of Temporal Dependence." In *Ecological Inference: New Methodological Strategies*, edited by Gary King, Ori Rosen, and Martin A. Tanner, 207–233. New York: Cambridge University Press.

R Core Team. 2018. *R: A Language and Environment for Statistical Computing*. Vienna, Austria: R Foundation for Statistical Computing. `www.R-project.org/`.

Rubin, Donald B. 1974. "Estimating Causal Effects of Treatments in Randomized and Non-randomized Studies." *Journal of Educational Psychology* 66 (5): 688–701.

Ruggles, Steven, J. Trent Alexander, Katie Genadek, Ronald Goeken, Matthew B. Schroeder, and Matthew Sobek. 2010. *Integrated Public Use Microdata Series: Version 5.0* [Machine-readable database]. Minneapolis: University of Minnesota.

Ruggles, Steven, Katie Genadek, Ronald Goeken, Josiah Grover, and Matthew Sobek. 2017. *Integrated Public Use Microdata Series: Version 7.0* [dataset]. Minneapolis: University of Minnesota. `https://doi.Org/10.18128/D010.V7.0`.

Särndal, Carl-Erik, and Sixten Lundstrom. 2005. *Estimation in Surveys with Nonresponse*. Hoboken, NJ: Wiley.

2008. "Assessing Auxiliary Vectors for Control of Nonresponse Bias in the Calibration Estimator." *Journal of Official Statistics* 24 (2): 167–191.

Särndal, Carl-Erik, and Imbi Traat. 2011. "Domain Estimators Calibrated on Information from Another Survey." *Acta et Commentationes Universitatis Tartuensis de Mathematics* 15 (2): 43–60.

Schickler, Eric, and Devin Caughey. 2011. "Public Opinion, Organized Labor, and the Limits of New Deal Liberalism, 1936–1945." *Studies in American Political Development* 25 (2): 1–28.

Splawa-Neyman, Jerzy. 1923. "On the Application of Probability Theory to Agricultural Experiments. Essay on Principles. Section 9." *Roczniki Nauk Roiniczych, Tom X:* 1–51. Reprinted in *Statistical Science*, 5 (4): 465–472, 1990. Translated from Polish by D. M. Dabrowska and T. P. Speed.

Squire, Peverill. 1988. "Why the 1936 *Literary Digest* Poll Failed." *Public Opinion Quarterly* 52: 125–133.

Stuart, Elizabeth A., Stephen R. Cole, Catherine P. Bradshaw, and Philip J. Leaf. 2011. "The Use of Propensity Scores to Assess the Generalizability of Results from Randomized Trials." *Journal of the Royal Statistical Society. Series A (Statistics in Society)* 174 (2): 369–386.

Tanner, Martin A. 1996. *Tools for Statistical Inference Methods for the Exploration of Posterior Distributions and Likelihood Functions*. 3rd ed. New York: Springer-Verlag.

Tibshirani, Robert. 1996. "Regression Shrinkage and Selection via the Lasso." *Journal of the Royal Statistical Society. Series B (Methodological)* 58 (1): 267–288.

Treier, Shawn, and Simon Jackman. 2008. "Democracy as a Latent Variable." *American Journal of Political Science* 52 (1): 201–217.

Valliant, Richard, Jill A. Dever, and Frauke Kreuter. 2018. *Practical Tools for Designing and Weighting Survey Samples*. Springer. PDF e-book.

Verba, Sidney, and Kay Lehman Schlozman. 1977. "Unemployment, Class Consciousness, and Radical Politics: What Didn't Happen in the Thirties." *Journal of Politics* 39 (2): 291–323.

Wagner, James. 2012. "A Comparison of Alternative Indicators for the Risk of Nonresponse Bias." *Public Opinion Quarterly* 76 (3): 555–575.

Wakefield, Jon. 2004. "Ecological Inference for 2 × 2 Tables." *Journal of the Royal Statistical Society. Series A (General)* 167 (3): 385–445.

Warshaw, Christopher, and Jonathan Rodden. 2012. "How Should We Measure District-Level Public Opinion on Individual Issues?" *The Journal of Politics* 74 (1): 203–219.

Weatherford, M. Stephen, and Boris Sergeyev. 2000. "Thinking about Economic Interests: Class and Recession in the New Deal." *Political Behavior* 22 (4): 311–339.

Wiseman, Frederick, and Philip McDonald. 1979. "Noncontact and Refusal Rates in Consumer Telephone Surveys." *Journal of Marketing Research* 16 (4): 478–484.

# Acknowledgements

First and foremost, we thank Mike Alvarez and Neal Beck for encouraging us to write this manuscript and shepherding it through the editorial process. We also thank Luis Campos, Michael Dougal, Luke Miratrix, Eleanor Powell, Mallory Wang, Chris Warshaw, and Ian Yohai, with whom we collaborated on related work. For research assistance, we are indebted to Dan de Kadt, Rob Pressel, Kathryn Treder, and Anna Weisman. For helpful comments, we thank Lucas Leeman. Finally, we gratefully acknowledge the financial support of the National Science Foundation (grants SES-0550431 and SES-1155143).

# Data Availability Statement

R scripts accompanying this Element are available at www.cambridge.org/Caughey and can be run interactively online via Code Ocean. Links for each section can be found below.

Section 1: https://doi.org/10.24433/CO.9047395.v1
Section 2: https://doi.org/10.24433/CO.3986927.v1
Section 3: https://doi.org/10.24433/CO.7194431.v1
Section 4: https://doi.org/10.24433/CO.0892243.v1
Section 5: https://doi.org/10.24433/CO.0010101.v1
Section 6: https://doi.org/10.24433/CO.5307324.v1

Cambridge Elements ☰

# Quantitative and Computational Methods for the Social Sciences

---



---

## About the Series

The Elements Series Quantitative and Computational Methods for the Social Sciences contains short introductions and hands-on tutorials to innovative methodologies. These are often so new that they have no textbook treatment or no detailed treatment on how the method is used in practice. Among emerging areas of interest for social scientists, the series presents machine learning methods, the use of new technologies for the collection of data and new techniques for assessing causality with experimental and quasi-experimental data.

Cambridge Elements

# Quantitative and Computational Methods for the Social Sciences

## Elements in the Series

*Twitter as Data*
Zachary Steinert-Threlkeld

*A Practical Introduction to Regression Discontinuity Designs: Foundations*
Matias Cattaneo, Nicolás Idrobo and Rocío Titiunik

*Agent Based Models of Social Life: Fundamentals*
Michael Laver

*Agent Based Models of Polarization and Ethnocentrism*
Michael Laver

*Images as Data for Social Science Research*
Nora Webb Williams, Andreu Casas, John D. Wilkerson

*Target Estimation and Adjustment Weighting for Survey Nonresponse and Sampling Bias*
Devin Caughey, Adam J. Berinsky, Sara Chatfield, Erin Hartman, Eric Schickler, and Jasjeet S. Sekhon

A full series listing is available at: www.cambridge.org/QCMSS

Printed in the United States
By Bookmasters